The Virtual High School

TEACHING GENERATION V

The Virtual High School

TEACHING GENERATION V

Andrew Zucker and Robert Kozma

with Louise Yarnall, Camille Marder, and

Marnie Collier
Tracey Dove
Carlos Espinoza
Amy Lewis
Raymond McGhee
Kathryn Valdés
Kyo Yamashiro
Viki Young
Dan Zalles

TEACHERS COLLEGE PRESS

Teachers College, Columbia University
New York and London

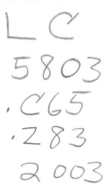
Much of the research on which this book is based was carried out as part of a contract with the Hudson (Massachusetts) Public Schools, as part of a grant made to Hudson Public Schools by the U.S. Department of Education for the development, operation, and evaluation of the Virtual High School, grant number R303A960571-98B.

Published by Teachers College Press, 1234 Amsterdam Avenue, New York, NY 10027

Library of Congress Cataloging-in-Publication Data

Zucker, Andrew A.
 The Virtual High School : teaching Generation V / Andrew Zucker and
Robert Kozma with Louise Yarnall, Camille Marder, and associates.
  p. cm.
 Includes bibliographical references and index.
 ISBN 0-8077-4286-4 (pbk. : alk. paper) — ISBN 0-8077-4287-2
(cloth : alk. paper)
  1. Distance education—United States—Computer-assisted instruction.
 2. Education, Secondary—United States—Computer-assisted instruction.
 3. Internet in education—United States. I. Kozma, Robert, II. Title.
 LC5803.C65 .Z83 2003
 373.133′4—dc21   2002028978

ISBN 0-8077-4286-4 (paper)
ISBN 0-8077-4287-2 (cloth)

Printed on acid-free paper
Manufactured in the United States of America

10 09 08 07 06 05 04 03 8 7 6 5 4 3 2 1

CONTENTS

FOREWORD

This book is a definitive study of an important emerging phenomenon: the use of virtual learning environments in U.S. pre-college education. The emphasis of *The Virtual High School* is on the most intensive example of K–12 learning-across-distance: virtual high school courses and programs. As the following chapters describe, the Virtual High School model (VHS) the authors studied is representative of the best aspects in distance education initiatives that now involve dozens of online schools and tens of thousands of students.

The organizations promoting these initiatives are varied. Many virtual high schools are encouraged and supported by the states in which they are located; quite a few began through substantial amounts of federal funding. Some programs are a product of private enterprise, while regional consortia sponsor others. These educational improvement efforts parallel comparable innovations occurring on an even broader scale in American higher education.

At the college level, where institutions can focus on learning without also having to fulfill the socialization and custodial care mandated for K–12 education, dramatic claims are being made about how much the advent of virtual teaching and learning will undercut face-to-face educational experiences. Thus far, most of those predictions are unfulfilled, but even critics concede that distance-learning experiences are a permanent addition to the fabric of higher education. This book explores the possibility that similar structural shifts leading to the routine inclusion of learning-across-distance may develop in K–12 settings.

As the authors document, the benefits claimed for virtual high school courses include:

- preparing 21st-century students for fluent use of interactive media in knowledge-based workplaces;
- providing access to courses not available locally, as well as to remote archives and distant experts;
- delivering instructional offerings at lower cost with reduced administrative overhead;
- using teaching strategies that build on the learning styles of kids growing up in a media-intensive world; and
- involving excellent instructors attracted by the opportunity both to offer courses they otherwise could not teach and to employ pedagogical strategies difficult to use in traditional classroom settings.

This longitudinal evaluation provides both conceptual frameworks and empirical data for determining the veracity of those claims.

Critics also charge that virtual learning experiences at the pre-college level have a number of disadvantages, such as exacerbating the gap in educational outcomes between "haves" and "have-nots"; providing inadequate instruction for some types of content, such as foreign languages or science laboratories; dehumanizing the process of learning for both students and teachers; requiring self-discipline and internal motivation that many students don't have; and creating additional challenges for the already overburdened profession of teaching. Documenting the extent to which these concerns are justified even in the best of current implementations, this study provides a balanced perspective on the evolution of virtual high school courses and programs.

In creating and refining the VHS project, the organizational model that the Concord Consortium and its collaborators developed is generalizable to many distance education settings. Its innovative features include:

- the use of multiple institutional participants to distribute the investments and costs associated with virtual high school courses,
- extensive professional development for participating teachers, centered both on course development and on delivery,
- innovative pedagogies for distance-based courses that go beyond automating and virtualizing conventional instruction,
- the involvement of trained coordinators at every implementation site, and
- a sophisticated evaluation process, with results triangulated across multiple methods and metrics.

The analysis of the model provided in this book is invaluable for anyone seeking to develop virtual learning experiences at any developmental level, in any context.

The process the investigators use to conduct this analysis of strengths and limitations is also an important contribution to education research. The more we understand the complexities of fostering learning (at both individual and organizational levels) within the constrained settings of conventional schools, the more intransigent the barriers appear to achieving substantial educational gains for all students. One problem frequently encountered is that research insights reveal opportunities for considerable improvements possible in theory, but almost impossible to actualize under current conditions of practice. As one illustration: a "reform" movement based on broad, shallow content coverage measured via low-level summative assessments has made the research-based pedagogical strategies advocated in the National Academy of Sciences report, *How People Learn* (Bransford et al., 2000), very difficult to implement.

Scholars and practitioners face a second problem in attempting to transfer an educational intervention promising in some school settings. Because of the strong influence of local contextual factors on any educational process, modifications in both the research-based intervention and its new settings-of-usage are essential for success outside the initial site. However, conventional research methods provide few insights into understanding and implementing this process of adaptation, and also typically marginalize educators and policy makers as mere consumers of scholarly insights, so such improvement strategies generally fail to surmount the challenge of "scaling up."

Design-based research is an emerging model of scholarship that may surmount some of these problems. As described in Hoadley (submitted for publication), design-based research centers on creating knowledge about developing and sustaining innovative learning environments based on theoretical claims about teaching and learning. This involves practitioners and researchers working together to produce meaningful change in contexts of practice (e.g., classrooms, after-school programs, teacher online communities), with goals and design constraints drawn from the local context as well as the researchers' agendas. Viewing both the design of an intervention and its specific enactments as objects of research demands a methodology that can document and account for the contextual interdependence of design and setting, produce robust explanations of innovative practice, and provide localizable principles for others to apply to new settings. The development of the VHS model, formatively shaped by its ongoing evaluations, is one of the most detailed, best constructed examples of design-based research to date, making a valuable methodological contribution to all forms of theory-driven educational innovation.

The VHS model also is a potential precursor to a broader evolution in education that combines the best aspects of classroom interactions and distance education. "Distributed learning" is a term used to describe educational experiences that combine the use of face-to-face teaching with synchronous and asynchronous mediated interaction. This instructional strategy distributes learning across a variety of geographic settings, across time, and across various interactive media. Our research (Dede, Whitehouse, & Brown-L'Bahy, in press) shows that the integration of interactive media into learning profoundly shapes students' educational experiences.

Many students report that the use of asynchronous learning environments positively affects their participation and their individual cognitive processes for engaging with its content. In addition, students indicate that synchronous virtual media both helped them get to know classmates with whom they might not otherwise individually interact within a classroom setting and provided a clear advantage over asynchronous media in facilitating the work of small groups. These findings have implications for the instructional design of both conventional distance education and traditional classroom instruction. In particular, the evolutionary inclusion of more synchronous media into the VHS model may address problems this study cites of dropouts, low student-to-student interaction, and minimal transfer of insights from online teaching into the classroom instruction of high schools implementing distance learning courses and programs.

Overall, as the authors discuss in their final chapter, the VHS model and learning-across-distance in general have not yet realized their full potential. Beyond implementing the "lessons learned" described in this study, virtual courses and programs can soon take advantage of a variety of new interactive media. Over the next decade, three different kinds of interfaces and infrastructures for distributed interaction will become increasingly important.

The first interface is the familiar notion of "bringing the world to the desktop computer." Via Internet2, broadband and collaboration technologies are becoming much more powerful, enabling increased interaction with distant experts and archives. In contrast, the second interface is "ubiquitous computing" via wearable wireless devices. The metaphor is not sitting somewhere and having the technology bring things to you, but instead being able to wander through the real world with the virtual world superimposed through "smart objects" and "intelligent contexts" (Dede, 2002). The third interface takes users "through the looking glass" of the computer monitor into a virtual context with digital artifacts, participants' avatars, and computer-based agents. One example of research on shared virtual environments would be the studies of a simulated historical setting I and my colleagues developed for teaching science to middle school students (*http://www.virtual.gmu.edu/muvees*).

The confluence of these three complementary types of interfaces is enabling experiences for this generation of students, experiences radically different than anyone has had to date. Models such as VHS are an important stepping-stone toward an educational future that takes full advantage of almost magical capabilities for sensing, acting, and learning across barriers of distance and time. This book provides deep insights into the current strengths and limitations of the best of these models.

Chris Dede
Harvard Graduate School of Education
July '02

References

Bransford, J., Brown, A., & Cocking, R. (2000). *How people learn: Brain, mind, experience, and school*. Washington, DC: National Academy Press.

Dede, C., Whitehouse, P., & Brown-L'Bahy, T. (in press). Designing and studying learning experiences that use multiple interactive media to bridge distance and time. In

C. Vrasid & G. Glass (Eds.), *Current perspectives on applied information technologies. Vol. 1: Distance education.*

Dede, C. (2002). Augmented reality through ubiquitous computing. *Learning & Leading with Technology, 29*(8), p. 13.

Hoadley, C. (submitted for publication). *Design-based research: An emerging paradigm for educational inquiry.*

PREFACE

In 1996, when SRI International was commissioned to evaluate the Virtual High School,[1] few people were predicting the great speed with which virtual schooling for secondary students would catch on. Six years later, there are dozens of online schools—including many authorized by governors and state legislatures—and tens of thousands of high school students are taking courses every year through the Internet. It is rare for education systems to change so quickly, and particularly "from the inside."

In hindsight, we might have been prepared to expect more rapid change among secondary schools based on the experience of postsecondary education institutions. Teaching and learning through the Internet are now quite common in colleges and universities. Currently, nearly 10% of all postsecondary institutions in the United States—meaning many hundreds of them—offer entire certificate or degree programs through the Internet, and far more offer some number of Internet-based courses, but not whole programs. Yet the very speed at which change has been taking place, both in higher education and in high schools, means that it has been difficult to stay up-to-date about what is happening. Despite the fact that far more students now enroll in online courses at the postsecondary level than at the high school level, the increasing prevalence of online schooling at both levels has taken place more or less simultaneously, namely, during the past decade.

Although we would not have been very good prognosticators 6 years ago, nonetheless our increasing awareness of the growth and popularity of virtual schools was the main impetus to write this book. We realize that the great majority of high school principals, students, and parents are likely to know little about online schools. School board members, too, who often need to approve a school district's participation in such ventures, have had limited opportunities to learn about these new institutions from close observation, simply because such a small percentage of high school students has been enrolled. Providing a thorough, detailed account of online schooling has been our primary goal in writing this book.

----

1. The name Virtual High School and the acronym VHS are trademarked by the Concord Consortium (based in Concord, Massachusetts), a co-developer of VHS with the Hudson (Massachusetts) Public Schools.

As we published evaluation reports about the Virtual High School over the years, we also became aware that good research about online schooling is hard to find. "There is a relative paucity of true, original research dedicated to explaining or predicting phenomena related to distance learning," concluded one research review (Institute for Higher Education Policy, 1999, p. 2). The same report also noted that "the overall quality of the original research is questionable and thereby renders many of the findings inconclusive" (p. 3). Some additional research has been published since 1999, but not enough. Furthermore, we have observed, as have others before us, that there is a tendency among some authors to publish information only about the positive aspects of online education. Yet a balanced perspective is vital. It is critical that researchers report not only about the considerable successes of online schools but also that the research clearly identify and document problems so that they can be better understood and, whenever possible, solved. Thus, a second goal for this book is to fill some of the gaps in research that currently make it difficult to get a thorough understanding of the strengths and weaknesses of virtual schooling.

Because SRI has studied the Virtual High School since its inception, we have accumulated an enormous amount of research-based information about the school and its participants. It was our good fortune to be able to study this particular technology innovation in such depth. Among the 99 Technology Innovation Challenge Grants made by the U.S. Department of Education, the one awarded to the Concord Consortium that started the Virtual High School has turned out to be perhaps the most successful and best known. Indeed, we are familiar with many federal grant programs, and it is no exaggeration to say that the award the government made to start the Virtual High School is that special, one grant in a thousand that becomes known to countless people, located in nearly every state and around the world.

Yet no matter how successful the Virtual High School, or any online school, has been to date, the development of virtual high schools is still at an early stage. There will be a great many changes in the coming years—technologically, organizationally, and in other ways. The final goal for this book is to assist policy makers at all levels as they create, adapt, and learn how to effectively use the new online schools. We hope that the intent and the result of such actions is to strengthen the public education system.

ACKNOWLEDGMENTS

This book is based on a 5-year evaluation of the Virtual High School carried out by staff at SRI International (an independent, not-for-profit research and consulting organization) beginning in 1996. Funding for the Virtual High School project, including funds for the evaluation, came principally from a Technology Innovation Challenge Grant (# R303A960571-98B) awarded to the Hudson Public Schools by the U.S. Department of Education. However, the opinions, findings, conclusions, and recommendations in this book are those of the authors and do not necessarily represent the views of either the U.S. Department of Education or the staff of the Virtual High School. We appreciate the support provided by the U.S. Department of Education.

The principal investigators for the Virtual High School, Dr. Robert Tinker (president of the Concord Consortium) and Dr. Sheldon Berman (superintendent of the Hudson Public Schools) have been supportive of our work from the outset—beginning even before the Challenge Grant was awarded, while the proposal was in its development stages. It is difficult at times to allow third-party evaluators to investigate and report on a budding, growing, challenging project, providing them with the freedom to document problems and shortcomings, as well as accomplishments and successes, and then to report their findings to sponsors and to the wider world. We very much appreciate the integrity, honesty, and courage of all of those involved with the Virtual High School who allowed us to work with them so closely and to "call it as we see it," reporting both what worked well and what did not. Their willingness to face and to overcome problems made our work possible. In addition to Drs. Tinker and Berman, many others worked closely with us over the years. Special thanks are due to Elizabeth Pape, now CEO of the Virtual High School, who was our liaison with the project. We also want to recognize Bruce Droste, Ray Rose, Steve Walsh, Storie Walsh, and many others who helped us, provided constructive criticism, and responded to our repeated requests for assistance.

Site visits took place in nine schools that were part of the Virtual High School consortium. We are indebted to the principals, teachers, site coordinators, and students at these schools, and particularly to the teachers who let us peer over their shoulders, virtually speaking, as they learned to teach a new course online, including: Pam Martin and Cynthia Costilla (Allen High School, Texas), Billy Millican (Dade County High School, Georgia), Thomas Redding (Ellet High School, Ohio), Ed Elberfeld (Fort Hayes Metropolitan Education

Center, Ohio), Karen Deavers and Peggy Collins (Hudson High School, Massachusetts), Anita Bergh and Tony Scalia (Kennedy High School, California), Terry Haugen (Miramonte High School, California), Kevin Johnston (New Hanover High School, North Carolina), David Jost and Tracy Sheehan (Westborough High School, Massachusetts). Over the years, literally thousands of students, hundreds of teachers, and dozens of school principals and superintendents also responded to questions and surveys. Thanks are due to all of them.

At SRI International, many researchers, programmers, editors, and others contributed their energies, know-how, and dedication to collecting, analyzing, and reporting about the Virtual High School. In addition to the four authors listed on the cover, we appreciate the contributions of Marnie Collier, Tracey Dove, Carlos Espinoza, Amy Lewis, Raymond McGhee, Kathy Valdés, Kyo Yamashiro, Viki Young, and Dan Zalles. Bonnee Groover, Klaus Krause, and Robin Post at SRI also helped in preparing this book, as did Chrisanne Gayl, a student associate at SRI. Thanks to all the members of this productive team.

Chapter 1

ONLINE LEARNING AND EDUCATIONAL CHANGE

Just a decade ago, the notion of offering high school courses on the Internet seemed futuristic and utopian. Yet today thousands of Americans log on to take high school foreign-language courses, special electives such as philosophy and art history, advanced placement classes in calculus and chemistry, full menus of general courses leading to diplomas, and even physical education. Hundreds of secondary teachers are signing up to "go virtual," attending Web development classes and studying the fine points of teaching students with mouse, keyboard, and screen instead of chalkboard and chalk.

From 1996 to 2002, at least a dozen state departments of education have created statewide virtual high schooling services. In half a dozen more states, regional education consortia have begun offering online high school classes. Several private enterprises, each drawing tens of millions of dollars in venture capital, have emerged to cater to this new market. Three longtime high school correspondence schools for adults and teenagers now offer programs online. A handful of charter virtual high schools have sprung up, too, opening up a potentially lucrative learning frontier that has brought together such unlikely bedfellows as William Bennett, the former secretary of education known for his advocacy of moral education, and Knowledge Universe, the educational venture led by former junk bond trader Michael Milken, who was convicted of securities fraud in 1990. The rapidity of the evolution of virtual high schooling from a mere gleam in the eye to a diversified system of online high school educational programs with devoted adherents has been stunning.

This book examines the phenomenal growth of virtual high schooling through the lens of one of the pioneering efforts—the Hudson Public Schools–Concord Consortium Virtual High School (VHS). Begun as an experiment in the mid-1990s with a $7.4 million grant from the U.S. Department of Education, VHS experienced rapid growth and impressive success, as did other virtual high schooling pioneers. Over the first 4 years of operation, the number of semester credits awarded annually to students taking VHS courses leapt from 700 to more than 3,000. The number of courses offered increased from 27 to about 150. School superintendents, principals, teachers, and students overwhelmingly expressed their satisfaction with VHS and their interest in continuing in the program, even though it took more time and cost more money than they had originally anticipated.

The book also examines the implications that online schooling has for the future of education, again through the lens of VHS. Does the rapid emergence, growth, and acceptance of virtual high schools portend significant change in the structure and delivery of education in the future, or will some late-21st-century historian or archeologist unearth this "innovation" while digging through the scrap heap of failed educational reforms? What are the factors that work for and against lasting educational change?

The book draws on 5 years of evaluative research that includes surveys of dozens of superintendents and principals and hundreds of teachers and students. As members of the evaluation team, we conducted interviews with teachers, convened focus groups with their students, and "virtually" peered into their classrooms. We conducted follow-up interviews with former students, who reflected back on their VHS experience from the perspective of college or work. We worked with panels of experts who established criteria for excellent virtual courses and applied them to a sample of VHS courses. We compared virtual courses with their face-to-face equivalents. We talked to leaders of the Virtual High School program and to other pioneers in the virtual-school movement. What we found provides insight into this important development, why it has been successful, and the promise it holds for the future. But our findings also identify problems with online learning and speak to the difficulty of changing the current educational system.

The Promise (and Problems) of Technology for Educational Change

Over the decades, many communications-based innovations have hit the educational scene, often with great fanfare and promise. Going way back, the U.S. Postal Service inspired the creation of correspondence courses in the 1880s. At the time, it was predicted that:

> The day is coming when the work done by correspondence will be greater in amount than that done in the classroom of our academies and colleges, when the students who shall recite by correspondence will far outnumber those who make oral presentations. (quoted in Simonson, Smaldino, Albright, & Zvacek, 2000, p. 23)

Since then, educators have adapted each new communication technology, from broadcast radio and television to two-way video, to the needs of distance learning (Farrell, 1999; Morabito, 1997). Often these new technologies were introduced with the same claims for dramatic change as were stated in the 1880s. Thomas Edison said of his newly invented motion picture technology that it "is destined to revolutionize our educational system and that in a few years it will supplant largely, if not entirely, the use of textbooks" (quoted in Tyack & Cuban,

1995, p. 111). In the long term, however, these technologies have had limited impact on the typical high school. By contrast, online technology seems to be poised to appeal to a much broader segment of the high school population than any previous technology. Will it? What is the promise of online learning? What are the problems and issues in its use? Will this new technology go the way of other fads, or will it change the way teaching and learning are done?

Benefits Claimed for Online Learning

At a policy level, the claims for online learning have often been framed in terms of promoting U.S. global economic competitiveness and preparing students for the 21st-century information economy (Information Infrastructure Task Force, 1993; President's Committee of Advisors on Science and Technology, 1997; U.S. Department of Education, 1996). The argument goes that students' use of computers will give them technological skills they will need in the new economy. Finding and using information on the World Wide Web will help students develop the cognitive skills needed to search for, organize, analyze, and use information to create "knowledge products," skills needed by the "symbolic analysts" of the new economy (Reich, 1991).

But beyond improving national competitiveness and the global economy, the benefits of online learning have often been examined in terms of the needs of students, teachers, and schools. For example, many writers have touted the benefits of online learning for educational access (Harasim, Hiltz, Teles, & Turoff, 1995; Hiltz, 1995; Web-Based Education Commission, 2000). Their argument is that the Internet can be used for access to education from anywhere at any time. Often, the claim is prefaced by the phrase *the best*, as in access to *the best* teachers, schools, and courses. Quality is an important aspect of this claim. As one superintendent put it in an interview, "Without quality, there is no virtual high school." Currently, more than 50 million school-aged children in the United States have access to education of some sort. The Internet, so the advocates claim, will provide them with access to better education.

But claims of access go beyond just those of access to good teachers and courses. It is also claimed that students and teachers will have access to other people that they would not otherwise be able to communicate with—people in other locations and occupations. That is, the Internet allows students and teachers to communicate with experts, politicians, scientists, businesspeople, and students and teachers in other parts of the country or world. Students will also have access to millions of documents, databases, libraries, museums, and other online resources as more and more information goes on the Web.

The access afforded by online learning also extends education to students with special needs. Students who are homebound, live in rural areas, or are disabled can have access to teachers and other students that they would not have otherwise. Working adults or prisoners could finish high school when they could not do so otherwise because of limitations of time or place. Students who, because of first language, race, gender, or other circumstances, are uncomfortable participating in classroom discussions may be emboldened by the relative anonymity of the electronic classroom and feel free to participate equally with other students.

In addition, a number of pedagogical advantages are often claimed for online learning (Harasim et al., 1995; Hiltz, 1995; Knowlton, 2000; Palloff & Pratt, 1999, 2001). Although online education does not *necessarily* bring with it new ways of teaching and learning, advocates see the Internet as an opportunity to introduce or reinforce a number of improvements in pedagogical practice. For example, the fact that students can choose what and when they want to study pushes online instruction toward a more active, "student-centered" pedagogy, focusing more on what students want to learn than on what teachers want to teach. It also supports self-paced, individualized learning—instruction that addresses the students' specific needs and allows them to progress at their own rate. As a result, so the claim goes, students become more autonomous and independent learners.

While some advocates emphasize a stronger connection between the individual learners and their use of instructional resources, others (Palloff & Pratt, 1999, 2001) emphasize the social aspects of online learning. The networked classroom supports collaborative learning and allows students distributed all around the United States to work together in groups with shared resources and on joint projects. It introduces them to new people and new perspectives that they may not encounter otherwise. The asynchronous nature of most online learning allows students to be more thoughtful in their discussion and to think more deeply about a topic. At the same time, the arrangement frees teachers to spend more time interacting with individual students rather than the whole class.

Online learning also is seen as a boon for school administrators (Twigg, 1994; Van Dusen, 2000). The Internet, it is claimed, can reduce the costs and increase the efficiency of instruction:

> The availability of a vast quantity of learning materials easily accessible via the network will make possible the creation of new kinds of learning environments. By lessening the need for direct faculty intervention in the learning process and increasing the ability of students to find and use learning materials on their own, we can create more-cost-effective instruction. (Twigg, 1994, p. 3)

In addition, the accessibility of online courses allows schools to provide their services to a larger market of students. A broader audience can create more enrollments and support a larger, more diverse curriculum, which, in turn, might create more student interest.

Teachers presumably benefit from online learning as well (Collison, Elbaum, Haavind, & Tinker, 2000). It allows them to take on new roles as mentor or facilitator, rather than lecturer or performer. The expanded student market accessible through the Internet allows teachers to teach courses that they would not be able to offer otherwise. And this same network connects teachers to resources, experts, and other teachers who can support their professional development and their online course efforts.

Reported Limitations of Online Learning

However, these same advocates are quick to say that online learning is not suited for every person, course, or situation (Harasim et al., 1995; Hiltz, 1995; Palloff & Pratt, 1999, 2001). It has its problems and limitations.

Some of these problems are the flip side of the highly touted advantages of online learning. Take access, for example. There are those who feel that an educational "digital divide" is growing between people who have access to computers and high-bandwidth networks and those who do not (Web-Based Education Commission, 2000). In fact, it is quite clear from a U.S. Census Bureau report (Newburger, 2001) that computer access at home varies with such factors as age, race, education, and income. For example, in the year 2000, about 88% of adults in households with yearly family incomes of $75,000 or more had a computer at home, compared with only 34% of those with incomes below $25,000. Similarly, 76% of people with a bachelor's degree or higher lived in a household with a computer available, compared with only 18% of those without a high school diploma. It seems that certain classes of people are less able than others to take advantage of the new resources that are available through the Internet.

Even when students have access to the equipment and networks, some may be disadvantaged. Students who have limited technology skills may find the use of the required hardware and software cumbersome and intimidating, even if they use tutorials to learn how to use computers or receive other forms of assistance. Students who have limited literacy skills may have difficulty relying on information that is still, for the most part, text based. But even literate students are confronted with problems if their language does not happen to be English. One study (Alis Technologies, 1997) estimated that 84% of the content on the World Wide Web is in English, 1.2% is in Spanish, 1.5% is in French, and 1.6% is in Japanese. Most other languages did not even appear in the results of the study.

The new pedagogy fostered by online learning may also be a problem for some students. The autonomous learning style supported—perhaps demanded— by online courses may require a high degree of motivation and benefit only those students with strong study skills and habits. Other students may have difficulty handling the delayed feedback that is part of asynchronous communication. They may have trouble staying on task and keeping up. Studying any place, any time may become studying at no time for those who lack the academic discipline. Dropping out may be the real outcome for these virtual students.

Teachers may also find that there are disadvantages. Do they lose control over the content, pedagogy, and student contact within their courses? Do they find that online teaching responsibilities are layered on top of other responsibilities, as administrators seek to use this approach to create efficiencies and save money?

The Internet may not be a good way to teach certain kinds of courses. Learning to speak a foreign language requires speaking with others, a capability not currently built into most online course technologies. Similarly, it is difficult or cumbersome to generate mathematical symbols or other kinds of special graphics in some online environments, and this capability is essential for certain courses. Hands-on courses, such as laboratories, also might be difficult to replicate online.

Finally, some critics cite the dehumanizing potential of online courses. Students are left to form a close bond with their computer while a distance is created between them, their teachers, and other students.

Where do online courses fall between nirvana and anathema? Are they panaceas or fads? In our research, we found reasons to be exuberant and also reasons to be concerned. But the creators of the Virtual High School and other pioneering online efforts were first inspired by the Internet's tremendous potential to support educational change and improvement.

Origins of the Virtual High School

Although the story of VHS, like other online education ventures, has an intensely personal side, it is useful to view its origins in the context of the larger story of technological proliferation in the late 20th century. Against this backdrop, the rapid growth of virtual high schooling seems to be an extension of Moore's law, further proof that innovation and adaptation grow exponentially with each new invention in information technology.

Computers and the Internet

It took 50 years from the end of World War II to the eve of the second millennium for computing machines to evolve from bulky, room-sized apparatuses designed to calculate military firing tables to the compact, typewriter-sized devices found in a third of American homes, half of American workplaces, and nearly every classroom serving American students (Newburger, 2001; Weston, 1997). In less than 25 years—roughly half the evolutionary time of computers—the Internet grew from a top-secret military computer network designed to survive a nuclear first strike into a popular information system accessible at home to more than 37% of the American adult population, as well as in 98% of schools (Anderson & Ronnkvist, 1999; Newburger, 2001; National Center for Education Statistics [NCES], 2001b; Zakon, 2001). Its structural growth was astounding—from a network of about 160,000 Internet host computers in 1989 to 100 million host computers by 1999 (Zakon, 2001). In less than a decade—about half the time it took the Internet to grow—the World Wide Web developed from an information-swapping technology serving a close-knit community of Swiss particle physicists into a cultural tidal wave of 10 million Web sites (Zakon, 2001).

Distance Learning

Universities were the first to apply these new technologies to distance learning. Building on their existing organizational infrastructure, such as extension services and video-based courses, universities were quick to capitalize on this new medium. By the 1997–1998 school year, about one-third of U.S. colleges (both 2- and 4-year) and universities were offering distance education courses, with a total of more than 1.6 million enrollments (NCES, 2000). About 60% of these institutions used Internet-based instruction, more than used any other form of distance learning. Several states, such as California and Michigan, set up a virtual university to offer online courses, and the governors of 18 western states set up the Western Governors University, which uses the Internet and other technologies to offer degrees at the associate's, bachelor's, and master's levels.

Nationally, politicians and policy makers soon came to notice this phenomenon and its implications for K–12 education and other government services. In a bipartisan effort, the president and Congress marshaled the resources to build an "information superhighway" that rivaled the national effort of earlier years to build a network of roadways connecting the continent. An explicit goal of this effort was to increase access to high-quality education, to "the best schools, teachers, and courses . . . without regard to geography, distance, resources, or disability" (Information Infrastructure Task Force, 1993, p. 1). Congress also created a series of special programs that supported the use of technology in schools, among them Preparing Tomorrow's Teachers to Use Technology, Learning Anytime Anywhere Partnerships, Technology Literacy Challenge Fund, and Technology Innovation Challenge Grants. Started in 1995, the Technology Innovation Challenge Grants provided matching federal funding to partnerships of school districts, universities, businesses, research institutes, software designers, and others to promote the innovative uses of technology in schools.

Over the 5 years of the program, 99 five-year grants were given to school districts across the country, totaling more than half a billion dollars. VHS was funded by one of these grants.

The Virtual High School

On the personal side, the idea of the Virtual High School came up in 1995 during a lunch between Robert Tinker, president of the Concord Consortium, and Sheldon Berman, superintendent of Hudson Public Schools in Massachusetts. They felt that the Internet and the still-emerging World Wide Web held great potential for improving schools. Specifically, they felt that schools could use Internet courses to double or even triple their course offerings to meet the specialized needs of a wide range of students. They felt that netcourses could bring the world into schools by tapping the knowledge and experience of corporations, universities, and individuals anywhere. These resources could be used to accelerate students' advanced study in specialized courses. The Internet also could take the schools into the real world; these resources could be used to integrate students into work and society by providing them with academic support as they made their transition. Finally, they felt that netcourses could be used for teachers' professional development, aiding teachers at a distance to learn new content and adapt their teaching strategies to take advantage of the new medium. As a consequence, they felt that a virtual high school project could help schools to undertake significant educational reform.

Within the Concord Consortium, the idea of creating a virtual high school competed against dozens of other ideas at a 1996 staff retreat. The VHS idea was judged as having excellent potential. Tinker, Berman, and others then worked hard to assemble the right people and partners and write the winning grant proposal.

The goal of their project was to create a national consortium of schools that would expand members' curricular offerings through a wide range of excellent, current, innovative, network-based courses supporting reform (Tinker, 1996). This was to be done in a way that could grow and continue after funding ended, while spawning independent, parallel efforts. In their proposal to the U.S. Department of Education, Tinker and Berman stated five objectives for reaching this goal:

1. Create a large, diverse collaborative of schools that will share resources.
2. Provide high-quality, network-based professional development for participating netcourse teachers.
3. Develop and offer a wide range of excellent, innovative netcourses that take full advantage of the Internet and serve a diverse group of students.

4. Create a collaboration model that is feasible for all schools, scalable, and replicable.
5. Evaluate the project and its potential for wide-scale adoption.

With regard to the first objective, Tinker and Berman envisioned that the VHS Consortium would start with 50 charter member schools and would expand to a total of 130 during the 5-year project. This large scale would make it possible to offer specialized and innovative courses because, among them, these schools could provide both the faculty expertise and student demand. The project would act as a cooperative; each school would contribute the equivalent teacher time of at least one course and would be able to enroll a proportional number of students in network-based courses offered by VHS.

To assure the quality of the courses and the online learning experience—the second objective—Tinker and Berman proposed to offer their online teachers a rigorous professional development workshop on netcourse technology, techniques, and teaching practices. The workshop would be offered online and would be equivalent to a three-credit graduate course. All VHS teachers would be required to pass this course successfully before offering an online VHS netcourse. This requirement would assure students and schools that all netcourses were taught by well-qualified teachers who were well versed in the latest technologies, content, and teaching strategies.

The primary function of VHS is the third objective—to develop and offer a wide range of excellent, innovative netcourses. These would be offered to as many as 9,000 students over the 5 years of the project. Participating teachers, working in teams with assistance from experts, would adapt existing high-quality, standards-based course material to the netcourse format. The identification of courses to be developed would be informed by an annual needs assessment of all schools in the consortium. But a stated objective of the project was to develop courses for a full range of students. Five types of courses were identified in the proposal:

- Specialized courses for advanced students, particularly in mathematics, science, and languages, as well as introductory courses in fields such as psychology, economics, and engineering
- Technical courses in network operations that would give students highly marketable skills that they also could use to provide schools with technical support
- Innovative core academic courses, particularly those that would use network resources
- Courses that would support students in school-to-work programs

- Courses that would support students whose primary language was not English

It was proposed that these courses would take full advantage of evolving Internet resources and software. Students would use the Internet for collaborative research, access to experts in business and education, discussions with their virtual classmates, simulations, and publication of their work. Internet technologies would be incorporated that provided ways to make the Internet a more expressive medium for students with different learning styles, to simplify student tracking and evaluation, to handle registration and other administrative functions, and to provide adaptive aids to challenged students.

The fourth objective was to create a collaboration model that would be scalable, replicable, and feasible for all schools. The VHS Consortium was founded on the proposition that each school would contribute teacher time in proportion to the number of students they would enroll in netcourses. Tinker and Berman felt that this model inherently supported growth at no cost and could be easily transplanted to additional schools. Grant funds would be needed to launch this process, evaluate its feasibility, and provide assistance to poorer schools; but once begun and proven effective, the VHS Consortium could continue and be replicated without additional outside funding. The model would be feasible even in low-income schools because it made only modest hardware demands; schools could start with two computers and dial-up modems.

Finally, the fifth objective was to evaluate the project and its potential for wide-scale adoption. The project was to be thoroughly evaluated by an experienced, external team internationally recognized for its expertise in the role of technology in educational reform. The evaluation was designed to provide clear, ongoing documentation of success, highlight effective practice, and provide valuable lessons for others. The evaluation results, the consortium idea, the technology, and the netcourses were to be widely disseminated electronically, in print, and through professional presentations. This team of external evaluators from SRI International authored this book.

Other Online Schools

Other pioneering efforts to offer high school courses emerged alongside VHS. We collected and analyzed descriptive materials from several of these programs as well, and interviewed the pioneers who shaped their beginnings. Although we do not have the same depth of information on these programs as we do for VHS, we include these programs to provide a comparison and contrast with VHS and to extend our discussion of the implications of online learning for educational change.

Basically two kinds of organizations support the development of virtual schools: those, such as VHS, that offer virtual courses or programs (whether at the national, state, or local level) and those that provide the technologies and services that support these programs. IBM's Lotus Development Corporation, an example of the latter type of organization, produces LearningSpace, the technology used by the Virtual High School. This technology will be examined in detail in Chapter 3. A few organizations provide both courses and technology or services. Information about some of the organizations involved with virtual schooling, current as of fall 2001, is provided below.

Perhaps one of the most ambitious organizations to offer virtual courses is *Intelligent Education, Inc. (IEI)* of Atlanta, Georgia. IEI was founded in late 1999 to provide general education and elective courses at the high school level through the World Wide Web. The company uses technology developed by eClassroom to offer courses directly to students. The 98 courses are divided into two diploma programs, college prep and career technology. The courses were developed by teams of experts but are delivered online for independent study.

Class.com began in 1996 with a $2.5 million proof-of-concept grant from the National Science Foundation and a 5-year $15 million grant from the U.S. Department of Education Star Schools program. In 1998, program leaders decided to turn the program into a profit-making business. In recent years, they have raised more than $7.5 million in private investment and struck deals to offer courses to second-generation virtual high schools. Teams of teachers, curriculum specialists, and content experts have used technology from Blackboard Inc. to develop 28 courses in nine categories, such as math, science, social studies, and languages. The company markets to schools and school districts, offering to work with them to set up their own virtual schools using class.com courses and Blackboard technology.

CyberSchool began in Eugene, Oregon, in 1995 as an effort to provide supplemental courses online to high school students by establishing a network of participating districts across the United States. It now offers 48 courses through participating school districts in eight states. Teachers in these schools develop and offer courses, with CyberSchool guidance. Enrollments are limited to the participating states, and a significant portion of the tuition is returned to the schools offering the courses.

The Florida Virtual School (FVS) is a pioneer among a number of states (such as Alabama, Kentucky, Michigan, New Mexico, and about half a dozen others) that have begun their own statewide virtual programs. Started in August 1997 as the Florida Online High School, FVS began as a joint project between the Orange and Alachua County school districts, which incorporate the cities of Orlando and Gainesville, respectively. It has since expanded to include counties throughout the state. After partnering with IBM, the districts received a $1.3 million state grant to launch the program. FVS works with Florida schools and districts to offer 60 courses in a wide range of areas, including math, science, social studies, English, computer education, and physical education.

Apex Learning of Bellevue, Washington, received an estimated $40 million in start-up financing in 1997 from Microsoft co-founder Paul Allen, Edison Schools, and other sources. It initially focused on developing online advanced placement (AP) courses for high school students. For 2001–2002, Apex offered 16 courses in two areas: advanced placement and foreign languages. Online test preparation for AP examinations, another of their services, enrolls more students than the online AP courses themselves. Apex has also branched out to provide services and proprietary technology to school districts and state programs that are interested in developing their own virtual programs. Its clients include the Michigan Virtual High School and Houston Independent School District Virtual School.

Blackboard Inc. is one of several companies that do not offer courses but provide technology and services to companies, states, and school districts that want to develop their own virtual programs. Located in Washington, D.C., Blackboard was founded in 1997 to offer development and licensing services for online educational software. It has raised $100 million in investments from such partners as AOL Time Warner, Dell Computer, and Microsoft. Its primary market consists of Ivy League universities, public universities, community colleges, and international universities, but it also had contracts with at least 12 K–12 districts in the United States as of 2001, and at least two of these involved development of virtual high schools.

eCollege.com of Denver, Colorado, began offering online courses at the University of Colorado in 1996. It is a publicly owned company providing a variety of services to the online learning market, primarily the college market. It offers a portal that creates a Web-based virtual school environment and supports clients seeking to start their own virtual schools by providing server space, start-up consulting, courses, and course design support. In addition, it is offering online courses as supplements to regular face-to-face classrooms. In August 2000, the company established *eClassroom*, a division focused on developing online programs for the K–12 market. This division has partnered with the second-generation virtual high schools of Illinois, Kentucky, Matanuska–Susitna Borough School District in Alaska, and Gwinnett County Public Schools, the largest school district in Georgia.

There are dozens of online schools, most of them organized at the state or local level. As of early 2002, a project called the Distance Learning Resource Network (www.dlrn.org) maintained a Virtual School List providing links to as many schools as were known to them.

The extent and range of these virtual schools and services testify to the faith that people—both inventors and investors—have in this new technology and its ability to change education. But there are other forces—equally powerful (perhaps more so)—that constrain the ability of innovations to make fundamental and sustained change in education. It is to this part of the story that we turn next.

Tinkering Toward Utopia

In their book *Tinkering Toward Utopia*, David Tyack and Larry Cuban (1995) discuss a central tension inherent in American education—the tension between the intense faith that Americans have in education as an engine for social improvement and the gradualness of changes in educational practice. They capture this condition in the title of their book—the tension between the utopian vision inevitably set for education and the commonsense tinkering that most often characterizes actual change.

Tyack and Cuban looked across the history of educational change in the United States—changes that ranged from the introduction of common schooling and the Carnegie unit to the progressive education movement and the use of technology. They found that change is often initiated from outside the education system and is frequently accompanied by hyperbole and extravagant claims. The claims for the benefits of proposed reforms have run from preparing students for democracy and ending poverty and racial discrimination to developing the workforce for a new economy.

Would-be reformers would often buttress their calls for reform by excoriating the current state of education. The implicit—and sometimes explicit—culprit of the sorry state of education was invariably the teacher. Consequently, teachers were often excluded from the reform process, and some reforms were specifically designed to be "teacher-proof." Nonetheless, teachers were frequently the ones left to implement change. But rarely did they receive the additional time and resources that the reform required. More often than not, it was expected that these changes would be made on top of teachers' current responsibilities. If innovations failed or did not live up to their grand expectations—as was most often the case—teachers were frequently fingered as culpable.

Indeed, the U.S. educational system is extremely resistant to change, as Tyack and Cuban's historical analysis documents. But this situation is hardly the fault of teachers as a group. The structural organization of schools—what

Tyack and Cuban call the *grammar of schooling*—has proven extremely durable across many efforts to change it. The ways in which space and time are divided and credit is allocated, the sorting of students and their distribution to separate rooms, and the classification of knowledge into subjects, with grades awarded for performance, are all interlocking building blocks of what has come to be considered "real school." This structure has become the replicable, standardized way for handling large numbers of students and courses. As grand reform schemes were implemented over time and encountered the reality of the standard school grammar, they began to look much like the traditional way of doing things. In light of the utopian claims often made for these reforms, the resilience of the traditional school has been discouraging.

But change has occurred throughout the history of U.S. education. The standard school grammar does not work for everyone or in all situations. Modifications and adjustments have been made. Successful reforms, according to Tyack and Cuban, have typically been gradual and incremental—tinkering with the system.

Tyack and Cuban advocate a process of reform that works from the inside out, especially by enlisting the support and skills of teachers as key participants in reform. They view this approach as a positive kind of tinkering that knowledgeably adapts reform to local needs and circumstances, preserving what is valuable and correcting what is not. Under their approach to educational change, practitioners are enlisted from the start in defining problems and devising solutions. Reform policies are treated as hypotheses, and teachers are encouraged to create hybrids suited to their context, their needs, and the needs of their students. Instead of being ready-made plans, reform policies are formulated as principles or general aims that are embodied in practices that vary by school or even by classroom and that teachers modify in the light of experience. Such reforms are designed to be hybridized, to be adapted by teachers working together to take advantage of their knowledge about their own students and communities and supporting each other in new ways of teaching.

Under this hybridizing model of educational reform, a "successful" innovation may look quite different from school to school or classroom to classroom, or even different from what the reformers originally envisioned. With this approach, Tyack and Cuban contend that new curriculum frameworks, teaching methods, educational technologies, diagnostic tests, strategies for cooperative learning in small groups, and other innovations are best structured not as mandates from outsiders but as resources that teachers can use, with help from one another and outsiders, to improve student learning. Provided with the necessary time, money, and collegial support, teachers could work collaboratively with one another and with policy advocates, sharing goals and tactics and supporting one another in assessing progress and surmounting obstacles.

Such change is sometimes viewed as piecemeal or inadequate, but the authors claim that, over time, such revisions of practice, adapted to local contexts, can substantially improve schools. Rather than seeing the hybridizing of reform ideas as a fault, they suggest that it can be a virtue. Tinkering is one way of preserving what is valuable and reworking what is not. They contend that this approach has a far greater prospect for successful school improvement than mandates from above or from outside the school system.

We found that the observations of Tyack and Cuban rang true in the case of the Virtual High School. Hyperbole and exaggeration have certainly been common features of online learning and technology-based education reform, as noted previously. And although the Hudson–Concord VHS proposal was restrained in this regard, heightened claims were not altogether absent. The promise of technology to bring positive change was a strong personal motivator for the Virtual High School pioneers. But what we found in our 5 years of studying VHS was that when it succeeded—and it often did—it was less because of the touted advantages of technology and more because the approach taken by Concord and Hudson created a flexible program and built on the insight and energy of participating teachers. The basic structure of VHS was quite compatible with the standard school grammar, with its courses, credit hours, assignments, and grades. However, VHS technology and the flexibility of the program supported the tinkering of talented teachers to create and offer high-quality courses that otherwise would not have been available. The courses and policies that came to be implemented worked for teachers, students, and schools alike. VHS constitutes an authentic success story, when success stories about innovation are still rare in education, and it provides us with lessons learned that others can use as they venture into the world of virtual education.

Major Questions That Organize This Book

In this book we use our five-year examination of the Virtual High School to address many of the questions raised in this chapter. Specifically, the questions that follow organized our thinking and this book.

What is an online school like? How is an online school structured? What services does VHS offer to schools, teachers, and students? What are its course offerings? Does VHS include a full range of courses? Does it involve a full range of actual schools, including those from low-income or rural areas? Does it include a full range of students? Does the Virtual High School increase access to a wider variety of courses? Does it reduce costs? Can it scale to other schools? How is VHS similar to or different from other virtual programs?

What is the online course experience for teachers and students? What is it like to teach an online course? Is teaching an online course a lot of additional work? Who are the online teachers? How do they collaborate? What are the new roles that teachers take on? What kind of preparation is necessary to develop and offer an online course? What role do the teachers play in contributing to the success of the Virtual High School? What is the online classroom like? What is the difference between an online course and a similar course taught face to face? Are new kinds of pedagogies used? Is there more interaction between students and teachers and among students? What is the difference between an online course and a similar course taught face to face? What makes a good virtual course? Does online learning work for all kinds of courses?

What are the outcomes of a virtual school? How do administrators, teachers, and students like it? What do students value about the program, looking back at their experience? Do students learn special skills as a result of their experience? How does this learning compare with that in a face-to-face course? Does a virtual course foster active learning and self-direction? Does this independence work for all students? Does it increase student participation and community? What are the impacts on teachers and administrators?

What can be learned from the VHS experience? In what ways does the VHS structure contribute to success? What are the advantages and disadvantages of the technology used by VHS? Who succeeds in online schools? What is the importance of quality and quality control in a virtual school? What are the standards for online courses? How are these standards developed and implemented? What role does technology play in educational change?

These questions are addressed in the remaining chapters of this book. Chapter 2 introduces readers to the structure of the Hudson Public Schools–Concord Consortium Virtual High School and compares this structure with those of other online schools. It describes the range of course offerings in the VHS catalog and compares them with the types of course offerings provided by other virtual high school providers. We also characterize the schools, teachers, and students that have participated in the VHS program and draw on a case study of a typical high school to illustrate participants' activities in VHS, using the words of its superintendent, principal, teachers, and students.

In Chapter 3, we show what it is like to take and to teach an online course. We explain LearningSpace, the IBM Lotus technology that VHS uses to design and deliver its courses. We describe the structure of courses in this program and compare it with the structures of courses offered by other online programs. We illustrate this structure and technology with a case study of a VHS course. Drawing on findings from surveys, focus groups, and observations, we elaborate on this case with references to other VHS courses. We compare and contrast the characteristics of virtual and comparable face-to-face courses. We also discuss the characteristics of exemplary virtual courses.

Chapter 4 focuses on the various impacts of VHS. Drawing on our surveys and interviews, we examine the outcomes of participation in the program. We follow up on the experiences of several VHS students as they go on to other courses, college, or work. We look at the impact of VHS on student learning, persistence, and grades. And we examine the impact of the program on teachers and administrators.

Chapter 5 looks across our findings to analyze the successes—and failures—of VHS. We look at the components of the VHS model to assess why it works. We examine LearningSpace and other online technologies for their strengths and flaws. We draw conclusions about who succeeds in online schools. We look at the importance of quality control in VHS and the standards for online courses. Finally, we return to the issue that started us off, the role of technology in educational change.

Chapter 6 explores the reasons why virtual secondary education is growing, including the rapid spread of Internet technology, new requirements for raising education standards, the increasing demands for educational choice, and concerns about teacher shortages. Potential barriers to growth are also discussed. The future of VHS and other virtual schools is considered in light of preferences for competing approaches to the online secondary education market. The chapter and the book conclude with an examination of the likely impacts of future improvements in technology on virtual schooling and the connection between technological change and educational trends.

Chapter 2

THE VIRTUAL HIGH SCHOOL

When the Hudson Public Schools received a $7.4 million federal grant in 1996 to build the Virtual High School, co-principal investigators Shelley Berman (superintendent of Hudson Public Schools), Bob Tinker (president of the Concord Consortium), and their associates worked together as one of the first groups to design and then to operate a national online high school. The consortium arrangement that they used is distinctive among all the approaches that have since been adopted for online schools. By engaging teachers in dozens of regular high schools in the task of building and offering to a national audience NetCourses[1] they devised, the creators of VHS were able to strike a balance between managing a centralized, national effort, on the one hand, and stimulating a grass-roots engagement with a new approach to teaching by teachers in dozens of schools, on the other. Using a large group of teachers located in many states as the faculty for a virtual school is unusual, if not unique. Five years after the money was awarded, the "model" that the grant writers used to involve schools and teachers as partners still marks VHS as a pioneering effort.

The cadre of VHS teachers is just one of the vital components that make up the Virtual High School. Besides a group of excellent, hard-working teachers, other key components are the schools participating in the consortium, the students they enroll in VHS courses, and the site coordinators located in those schools. Perhaps the most visible component of the school is its catalog, which is easily downloaded from the VHS Web site (http://www.goVHS.org) and which, as of the 2001–2002 school year, includes more than 120 courses.

An additional component, as in any school, is a central administration. The VHS administration has certain familiar roles, such as enrolling students and making sure that there is a set of school rules that are understood, respected, and observed by all the participants. The VHS administration is also responsible for maintaining a technological infrastructure, including the servers on which its NetCourses are housed, and it is responsible for training new teachers to teach through the Internet. Overall course quality control is another task of the administrators, and it is one that we will return to several times in this book, because it is so important.

---

1. From this point forward, *NetCourse* or *VHS NetCourse* is used to designate online courses provided by VHS—that is, by schools participating in VHS—while *netcourse* is used to describe either online courses generically or specific online courses that are not provided by VHS.

Many of the components of VHS can be found in other virtual high schools or any other school: teachers, courses, regular high schools that allow their students to take online courses, central administration, and so forth. Yet the particular ways in which these components are conceived and structured vary among virtual schools. For example, the types of courses that are offered by different virtual schools vary considerably, as do the locations and roles of the online teachers, financial arrangements, and other elements.

The sections in this chapter describe each of the various components of VHS and how they work together. The experience of joining and participating in VHS is illustrated from the perspective of a participating school, Westborough High School in Westborough, Massachusetts. Then, after the Virtual High School is reviewed in detail, comparisons are drawn with other virtual high schools.

The Structure of VHS

The Virtual High School is structured as a cooperative, nationwide consortium of schools that pay a membership fee and provide teachers and courses to the system. Under this arrangement, schools gain access to a wide range of courses offered by teachers and schools nationwide. As of the 2001–2002 school year, member schools each pay a $6,000 annual membership fee. In exchange, for each NetCourse it offers, a member school receives 20 student seats per semester to the offerings in VHS's catalog of 120-plus courses. Member schools usually allow participating students to enroll in any VHS NetCourse they want (with sign-up from all the schools managed by the central VHS staff, including capping enrollments for each course, as needed), but they may counsel students about which courses meet particular requirements or may even restrict the students' choices to particular approved NetCourses. Because different students can enroll each semester, more than 20 students from a school often participate in a year. Several students from a given school may end up in the same NetCourse, but it is also possible that a student may be the only one from his or her school in a given course. In any event, the students in one NetCourse are typically located in many schools and multiple states, and the teacher may be in a school many miles away from most of his or her students.

Most of the NetCourses are one semester long and are offered twice each year. Teachers at consortium schools design and teach the courses in the catalog after paying to participate in one of two training programs, the Teachers Learning Conference or the NetCourse Instructional Methodologies course. Teachers are released from teaching one section of a face-to-face course (usually about 20% of a full-time teaching load) so that they can teach a VHS course. Each school also pays to train a school staff member as a site coordinator who monitors student participation, and the site coordinator also is released from about 20% of his or her normal duties to allow time to work with the VHS students.

VHS has offered alternative ways for schools to join the consortium. Initially, nearly all schools in the consortium housed a teacher who taught one NetCourse while the school enrolled up to 20 students each semester in other, distant schools' NetCourses. Over time, many schools have been interested in allowing some of their students to participate but have not been willing or able to commit a teacher to teach one section of a NetCourse. The current VHS policy is that if schools do not want to provide a teacher and course right away, they can gain access to the catalog for 10 students per semester by paying an $8,000 fee. Schools need to reapply for this option after each school year. Also, schools choosing to offer more than one section of a NetCourse receive a discount in the annual per-course membership fee, paying only $4,000 for each additional NetCourse. In return, they get an additional 20 slots for student enrollments in VHS courses (see Table 2.1).

Estimating a school's costs for participating in the program depends on several assumptions. Suppose that a school joins VHS with the expectation that it will stay in the consortium for at least 3 years and that during this time the same VHS teacher and site coordinator at the school will stay involved. Suppose, too, that the VHS teacher is released from teaching a face-to-face section that would have had an enrollment of about 20 students. Then the 20 students

Table 2.1
Summary of VHS Services, Requirements, and Fees

Services	Access to 120-plus course catalog for up to 20 students per semester; VHS central administration support; license for the teacher to use software tools.
Requirements	Computers with Internet access at school; one teacher to design and teach a course (20% full-time equivalent); one site coordinator to handle registration, grades, and student participation issues (20% full-time equivalent). Both the teacher and the site coordinator must take training provided by VHS.
Fees	$6,000 annually. One-time costs of $3,500 per teacher for an online professional development course and $1,500 per site coordinator for management training online. Optional: $4,000 and an additional course offering for an additional 20 student slots.

enrolled each semester in VHS courses account for the same number of student slots as are lost by the teacher dropping one face-to-face section, so there are no additional costs for the teacher per se. The program cost over 3 years would be $18,000 in annual fees ($6,000 per year), plus the one-time training fees for the VHS teacher ($3,500) and site coordinator ($1,500), for a total of $23,000 in cash payments to VHS, plus the cost of 20% of the site coordinator's salary. If we estimate the salary at $50,000 annually, then over 3 years the cost for the site coordinator's released time would be about $30,000. The bottom line is an additional cost of about $440 per participating student per semester. As one basis for comparison, given that per-pupil expenditures in public schools are now more than $6,000 annually and that high school students complete about six courses (or Carnegie units) each year, a face-to-face course costs about $500 per semester (assuming that all school costs are ultimately for the purpose of instructing students). Of course, the VHS costs are really an addition to the regular budget for participating schools and therefore may raise concerns.

Initially, VHS did not charge schools a fee to participate because the federal grant paid for VHS's costs. When asked in the fall of 2000 whether the additional resources used for students to take a VHS course were justified and acceptable, a majority of the principals in participating schools answered yes. At the same time, although they valued the very large course catalog that VHS makes available to them, more than 70% agreed that paying a $6,000 annual fee could be a significant barrier to continuing participation. VHS's administrators are aware that cost is a significant issue and are making an effort to reduce their fees. Despite the costs, about two-thirds of the VHS schools continued to participate after fees were instituted.

Participating Schools

In terms of size and location, schools that join the VHS consortium are typical of most other high schools. At the outset (the 1997–1998 school year), for example, the per-pupil expenditures, according to the district superintendents, averaged about $5,700, which was very close to the national average of $5,800 at that time. About one-quarter of the schools enrolled 500 or fewer students, while about one-third enrolled more than 1,200 students. By and large, these were typical schools. There were somewhat fewer rural schools than might have been expected, but access to the Internet was—and, in some cases, continues to be—difficult or expensive in rural areas. Nonetheless, schools with small enrollments may benefit most from VHS services, because they may be least capable of offering the range and number of courses that VHS provides.

By the 2000–2001 school year, VHS schools could be found in more than half of the United States as well as in several foreign nations. The great majority of the schools in the consortium continue to be regular, public, comprehensive high schools. A few are private schools. In their original proposal, Berman and Tinker suggested that VHS would be able to serve 130 schools by the end of the 5-year grant. In fact, the number of schools that are part of VHS grew from 27 in the first year to nearly 200 in the 2000–2001 school year. About 1,700 students were enrolled in VHS courses during the fall 2000 semester, and, because most VHS courses are one semester long, there were more than 3,000 course enrollments altogether in the fall and spring semesters that school year.

In nearly 70% of VHS schools participating in the 2000–2001 school year, more than 60% of students were taking college preparatory courses, and in more than half of the schools, fewer than a fifth of the students came from economically disadvantaged families. In almost two-thirds of the schools, fewer than 20% of students were racial or ethnic minorities—but in some schools, more than half the students were non-White. VHS schools with more than a few limited-English-proficient students were quite rare. This demographic picture of the VHS schools as a whole will be complemented by a description of the participating VHS students, which is provided in a later section of this chapter.

The major reason that schools chose to participate in VHS, according to the principals, was that VHS allowed them to offer courses that otherwise would not have been available to their students. Other reasons for schools' participation varied and typically were less important. In a few cases, for example, principals and superintendents were interested in exploring the use of technology in education and felt that VHS was a good choice. They believed that participation in VHS would fit into their technology plan, and some also thought that joining VHS would distinguish them from other schools. Some schools and districts also viewed the online medium's power for individualized mentoring as a way to help improve student performance, enhance educational equity, or provide more individualized instruction.

Interest in online courses springs from a variety of stakeholders within school systems. A growing number of parents and students increasingly see online courses as a way to obtain more one-to-one mentoring and a broader, more competitive range of specialized electives. Some online pioneers report being deluged with requests from teachers who see virtual schools as a way to teach from their homes, either permanently, such as after retirement, or temporarily, such as after the birth of a child.

VHS Teachers

VHS teachers are a highly educated and experienced group. All who responded to the fall 2000 survey had bachelor's degrees, and more than 75% had master's degrees; in addition, approximately 10% had educational specialist degrees or some other type of professional diploma. The corresponding figure for all American teachers is that only about 55% hold a master's or specialist's degree. Another distinguishing feature of this group is that they are willing, and often eager, to design a new course, which is an unusual activity for typical high school teachers. The evaluation team has referred to those attracted to VHS as "alpha teachers."

Nearly all VHS teachers have teaching certificates in their states for their main teaching assignments. Respondents to the fall 2000 survey had from 1 to 34 years of full-time experience, with an average of 16 years. The teachers were split evenly between males and females, but almost all were White. Out of 115 teachers who indicated their race/ethnicity, only one was African American and one was Hispanic.

For most VHS teachers, signing up to be part of the VHS experience was motivated by the ability to teach a course they had always wanted to design and teach. For others, it was motivated in part by a sense of challenge and adventure, particularly the notion of participating in an effort as technologically innovative as VHS. As put by a Texas teacher who teaches a course about various Hispanic cultures: "Just teaching is one thing, but teaching online is something else. . . . It broadens you. It's a new thing for me, and it's energizing to do something different—new and exciting. It's just been so much fun, and I'm so pleased that my school district agreed to go ahead and fund it."

The VHS teachers are given a lot of responsibility. Because the majority of them design a course that they have not taught before, materials for teaching the course must be written or found. Unless the resources are already available on the Web or are to be mailed to students (e.g., a textbook, or a set readings, or some hands-on materials for a science course), materials will need to be uploaded to the server that houses the NetCourses. Once the courses begin, teachers are expected to be online daily, or nearly that often, so that they can interact with their students. The teachers develop assignments, and they collect and grade students' work. They are asked to promote student-to-student interactions as well—for example, by asking students to collaborate on group assignments. As noted earlier, it is unusual for other virtual schools to place such a range of responsibilities on a widely dispersed group of teachers who continue to teach regular courses in their home schools. Indeed, in a few virtual schools, there really are no teachers, because the model is more one of self-study. In others, the online teachers are employed full time by the virtual school, becoming specialists in online teaching.

The Teachers Learning Conference

To help assure consistency in the quality of VHS NetCourses, VHS requires teachers to enroll in the Teachers Learning Conference (TLC), a 26-week online course worth 12 graduate-level credits that provides professional development in how to design and teach virtual classes, or the NetCourse Instructional Methodologies (NIM) course. The latter, which lasts only 15 weeks, is for teachers who will teach a section of an already-designed course. Both are intensive courses requiring 10 or more hours of work each week. By taking the TLC (or NIM) online, teachers get a foretaste of the kind of learning experience their own students will have. During these courses, teachers interact with VHS staff and one another about educational reform and issues related to the design and offering of virtual courses. As part of the TLC course, the teachers design a course that may be considered for inclusion in the VHS catalog. As noted above, the TLC or NIM course costs the member school $3,500 per teacher. A summary of the TLC syllabus is shown in Table 2.2. The range of topics in the course is great, with much of the focus on practical requirements for working effectively online. The NIM syllabus is similar but focuses less on course design.

Instructors in the TLC and the NIM have been selected primarily from staff of the Concord Consortium. They are experts in online course design and pedagogy and are able to draw on experience with a wide range of other Internet-based projects, in addition to what is now 5 years of working with VHS itself. In the year 2000, several of these experts published a book that summarizes much of what is known about effective online pedagogy (Collison, Elbaum, Haavind, & Tinker, 2000). An additional source of staff for the TLC and NIM courses is the pool of former VHS teachers.

The great majority of NetCourses begin with the interest and determination of potential VHS teachers. Usually, the subjects of NetCourses are chosen by the teachers who develop the courses. Through the TLC, central VHS staff provide the criteria and means to create an online course of high quality. With the help of TLC facilitators, teachers receive technical support, guidance, and feedback.

In the first 2 years of the VHS project, 20 to 30 potential VHS teachers were enrolled in the TLC each school year. Central VHS staff were able to keep close tabs on the progress of these teachers and improve on the TLC content. During the third year of the project, the number of teachers enrolled in the TLC grew to more than 100, and close monitoring of their progress became impossible for central VHS staff.

In an effort to continue to provide the guidance and feedback that had been available to a smaller number of teachers in previous years, the central VHS staff hired a number of TLC facilitators to mentor future VHS teachers in their new roles. During the 1998–1999 school year, facilitators were selected from a cadre of former and current VHS teachers who had experience developing NetCourses. In some cases, facilitators were teachers who had created exemplary NetCourses but, because of low student enrollment, did not deliver their courses during the school semester. Ideally, central VHS staff match 10 teachers in the TLC with one facilitator.

Table 2.2
Teachers Learning Conference Syllabus, 2000–2001

Week 1	Introduction to the virtual community
Week 2	Preparing the virtual environment
Week 3	Cooperating and collaborating virtually
Week 4	Using the Internet effectively
Week 5	Setting and applying standards
Week 6	Communicating in an online environment
Week 7	Managing the technology
Week 8	Refining the technology
Week 9	Providing and evaluating feedback
Week 10	Designing group activities
Week 11	Following the rules
Week 12	Adding graphics
Week 13	Practice assessing student work
Week 14	Developing a grading strategy
Week 15	More on grading
Week 16	Creating general grades, surveys, and assessments
Week 17	Personalizing required documents
Week 18	Administrative issues
Week 19	Retrieving tests, quizzes, surveys, etc.
Week 20	Self-assessment of your NetCourse
Week 21	Managing your course
Week 22	Sharing CourseRoom strategies
Week 23	Transitioning from design to delivery
Week 24	Investigating VHS resources
Week 25	Looking ahead to fall
Week 26	Graduation

Assessing Teachers in the TLC

Because the TLC is the arena in which potential VHS teachers develop the NetCourse curriculum, it is also an appropriate venue in which to assess whether teachers can successfully translate or prepare their courses for delivery online. VHS central staff hold teachers in the TLC accountable for completing development of at least the first 9 weeks of their VHS courses before allowing them to be offered in the VHS course catalog. NetCourses under development are expected to conform to standards developed under VHS's auspices (see Chapters 3 and 5); those that do not need to be revised or they will not be offered. In addition to course design and development, the TLC reviews innovative instructional methods as well as course expectations and VHS policies.

The fact that the central staff work closely with the potential VHS teachers during the TLC or the NIM course allows them to observe these individuals in action as well as to review the courses that are being developed. As a result of these observations and reviews, each year a few people are counseled out of the program before they become VHS teachers.

NetCourse Instructional Methodologies (NIM)

Beginning in the 1999–2000 school year, to meet the demand for certain course offerings, VHS began to supplement its focus on one-of-a-kind courses with a set of courses that are offered in multiple sections taught by different teachers. To prepare teachers to teach these courses, the special online training course, NetCourse Instructional Methodologies, was developed. Teachers can earn six graduate credits for the course.

VHS Students

Over the first 4 years of operation, VHS had more than 7,000 student semester enrollments in its courses. The demographics of the schools that choose to participate in VHS begins to tell the story of what these students are like. However, the students who participate in VHS, typically not more than 20 per school per semester, are only a small minority of the school's total student body. They are selected through a process that differs from school to school but that involves the students' choosing to sign up for particular VHS courses. Their involvement in VHS is usually reviewed by guidance counselors, VHS teachers, or the VHS site coordinator. Students who are not expected to succeed in an environment that requires a lot of independence are discouraged from participating. The great majority of VHS students are juniors or seniors, in part because younger students may not be ready for the responsibility of taking a course from a teacher hundreds or thousands of miles away. Some other virtual schools, such as the Florida Virtual School, have a considerably higher proportion of students enrolled in grades 10, 9, and even lower.

In fall 2000, according to site coordinators, 84% of VHS students were considered to be college preparatory, 17% were economically disadvantaged, and 20% were minority students. Only 3% were limited English proficient. Overall, then, the VHS students are similar to the other students in the schools from which they are drawn, except that the proportion of college-bound students is higher.

Students sign up for VHS courses mainly for the same reason that schools participate in the program—so that they can benefit from courses that otherwise are not available to them. Also, according to 86% of the students surveyed, they were attracted to VHS because "VHS courses are a very different way to learn," allowing them to log on at any time and from any place, including home. One student said:

> I wanted something more challenging [than the course available at her school], and I also wanted to try a virtual course. I liked the idea of a remote version and not being in class every day. . . . Independence fits my personality. This way of taking a course fits the way I am.

According to the fall 2000 student survey, 13% of the students were taking a VHS course as part of their core program, 56% were taking the course as an elective within their normal class load, and 31% were enrolled in the VHS course as an elective in addition to their normal class load. Although not all VHS students are able to enroll in the VHS course that is their first choice, the majority are.

The Catalog and the School Calendar

The VHS catalog is widely considered a basic resource for anyone embarking on a virtual high schooling initiative. It shows the breadth and variety of course choice that online technology can deliver to high school students and parents. Even a few examples from the first VHS catalog (1997–1998 school year) give a picture of the range at a time when the total number of courses offered (29) was relatively small: A Model United Nations Simulation Using the Internet, AP English: A Web-Based College Level Course in Literature and Composition, The Bioethics Symposium, Business in the 21st Century, Computer Technology I, Creative Problem Solving in Math & Logic, Current Issues in Nutrition and Health, Earth 2525: A Time Traveler's Guide to Planet Earth, Eastern and Western Thought—A Comparison, Explorando varios aspectos de culturas hispanas através del Internet.

Currently, VHS offers more than 120 courses. An alphabetical list of titles of NetCourses from the 2001–2002 VHS catalog is provided in Table 2.3. The full catalog, which is too long to be included in this book, includes course descriptions in addition to the titles.

Clearly, the catalog has grown and evolved in its offerings. In the initial VHS proposal, Tinker and Berman envisioned a balanced catalog featuring five types of courses: advanced courses in core subjects and professional fields, technical courses in technology, innovative academic courses, school-to-work courses, and courses for students whose primary language was not English. However, in the first year, VHS teachers did not choose to cover all subject areas and academic difficulty levels equally. The course selection favored advanced courses and one-of-a-kind, elective courses, while offering only sparse coverage of language courses and technical courses. VHS periodically asks member schools about the courses they would like and adds new courses accordingly. An effort also has been made to offer more courses for nonhonors and non-college-bound students, such as Career Awareness for the New Millennium, Rising Entrepreneurs, and many technical courses, such as Web Design. The result has been greater balance in the catalog. The Web Design course is an example of the recent VHS approach of offering multiple sections of popular courses. For 2001–2002, three sections of the course were available, each taught by a different teacher. Some VHS courses are labeled as honors level or advanced placement, but the great majority are standard level.

Most courses are one semester long and are offered in both the fall and the spring semesters. Fall courses start in September and finish in December. Spring courses start in January and finish in May. Students often choose to enroll in two VHS courses in a single year, one each semester. Although proponents of Internet-based courses sometimes talk of "any place, any time" access—and that is certainly possible with self-taught courses available on the Web—the VHS courses are carefully tied to school calendars. Teachers are also strongly encouraged to keep the students in their courses together on a schedule, if possible (an approach known as "scheduled asynchronous"), rather than allowing some students to zoom ahead while others procrastinate. In both respects—the calendar and the pace of the courses—VHS courses resemble traditional high school courses more than an independent study outside of a school.

Course Credit

Besides the selection of students who are allowed to participate in VHS, another local decision of importance is whether and how to award credit for VHS

Table 2.3

The VHS Course Catalog, 2001–2002

101 Ways to Write a Short Story	Contemporary Irish Literature
A Lifetime of Health & Fitness	Creating Art History
A Model United Nations Simulation Using the Internet	Current Issues in American Law and Justice
A Shakespeare Who-Dun-It	Democracy in America?
Academic Writing	DNA Technology
Aeronautics and Space Travel	Earth 2020
Algebra and Geometry	Eastern and Western Thought
American History	Economics
American Popular Music	Electricity and Electronics
Anatomy & Physiology	Employability Skills Section 1
AP Statistics Section I	Entrepreneurship
Aquaculture Science	Environmental Chemistry
Art and the Internet	Environmental Science
Art History	Environmental Science—The World Around Us
Artists and the 20th Century	Epidemics
Astronomy	Evolution and the Nature of Science
Aviation 101	Explorando culturas hispanas a través del Internet: Exploring Hispanic Culture
Bioethics Symposium	
Biology	
Biology II Section 1	Exploring the International Business World
Biotechnology	
Building in the New Millennium . . . Databases, That Is!	Exploring Themes in African-American Literature
Business and Personal Law	Film and Literature
Calculus for Business	Folklore and Literature of Myth, Magic, and Ritual
Calculus Made Simple	
Career Awareness for the New Millennium	Fractals
Careers	Genes and Disease
Chemistry II	Geology
Civil Liberties and the Constitution	German Cyber Adventure (Deutsches Cyberabenteuer)
Computational Science Using Java	Ghoulies, Ghosties, and Long-Legged Beasties
Constitutional Law	
Contemporary American Poetry	Gods of CNN: The Power of Modern Media

Table 2.3 (continued)

Hearts of Darkness	Pearl Harbor to the Atomic Bomb
Heroes Section 1	Personal Finance
History of Mathematics	Photography as Visual History
Information Technology Issues	Preveterinary Medicine
Integrated Mechanical Physics with Logical Reasoning	Project Sail
	Psychology II
Introduction to Programming in Visual Basic	Rising Entrepreneurs
	Same As It Never Was: Viewpoints on What Really Happened Throughout the Course of History
Investing in the Stock Market	
Is Romance Dead?: Love in Literature	
	Screenwriting Fundamentals
Kindergarten Apprentice Teacher	Shakespeare in Films
Learning to Invest in the Stock Market	Solving the Puzzle of English Grammar
Life, the Universe, and Everything	Survey of African American Literature/History
Literature of Charles Dickens	
Math in the Real World: Measuring the Earth	Technology and Multimedia
	The Holocaust
Math You Can Use In College	The Sunday New York Times
Mathematical Reasoning and Logic	The Vietnam War
Mathematics and Technology Connections	Time, Space, and Other Things
	To Kill a Mockingbird
Meeting America on the Appalachian Trail	Twentieth Century Women Authors
	Visual Basic 6.0
Meteorology	Walk on the Wild Side
Military History and Theory	Web Design and Internet Research
Multicultural Literature and Its Significance in Today's Society	Web Design
	Web Design: Web Paging the Great Scientists
Music Appreciation and Composition	
	WebQuest
Music Composition and Arranging	World Conflict, a United Nations Introduction
Music Listening and Critique	
Mythology	World Religions
Nuclear Physics	Writing and Telecommunications
Number Theory Section 1	Writing and the English Sentence
Parenting in the Twenty-First Century	
Peacemaking	

courses. The ways in which these decisions are made vary. Although it is common for schools to be faced with decisions about providing students with credit for courses not offered locally (many students transfer from other schools, for example), different states have different policies that affect local decisions.

In some states, it has taken time to adopt new policies. For example, during VHS's first year of operation (1997–1998), the curriculum director in the Allen Independent School District had to write a 90-page proposal to the Texas state education agency to get approval for offering the VHS courses and awarding credit to their students. Subsequently, the district reached an agreement with the state that decisions about providing course credit could be made locally, using established criteria. If the district assures the Texas Education Agency (TEA) of the quality of a VHS NetCourse, and if its description matches the description of a course already approved by the state, then the NetCourse can be offered for credit.

In contrast, at Kennedy High School in Fremont, California, all the courses were submitted to and approved by the school's normal course-approval committees. In this case, the district's superintendent felt that the process resulted in a buy-in for the VHS program by many teachers in the system. At Miramonte, another California high school, the courses had to be reviewed by a state university agency to classify them for the university's admission requirements. In this case, 25 of 30 VHS courses were approved, but 5 were not considered college preparatory courses. Schools are not required to award credit for every VHS NetCourse or to allow their VHS students to enroll in any particular online course they choose.

State and national standards for course offerings in elementary and secondary schools have become more visible and important in almost every state over the past decade. VHS tries to provide enough information about each NetCourse in its catalog so that decision makers are able to understand how the standards apply to the courses. The course titles, which are sometimes intended to be attention-grabbers, are supplemented by the longer course description and a syllabus. For example, Is Romance Dead? might bring to mind soap operas but is actually the title of a literature NetCourse that calls for students to read 15 to 20 pages each night, including works by classic authors such as Shakespeare, and to complete frequent writing assignments.

The process of obtaining approval for NetCourses now operates smoothly in most cases. Only 13% of the site coordinators reported having any difficulty getting their local school districts to approve courses for credit, and only 12% reported difficulties with their state education agencies. In the majority of those cases, the situation was resolved satisfactorily. Only 3% of the coordinators reported experiencing any difficulty obtaining approval from university systems in their states for VHS NetCourses taken by students.

Site Coordinators

In addition to enrolling teachers in the TLC or the NIM, a participating district or school also must commit to hiring a VHS site coordinator who serves as the point of contact for administrative matters and as a monitor for student participation, registration, and grading. The site coordinator can be a teacher or other school employee who spends one period a day coordinating the participation of the school's VHS students. As noted above, new site coordinators must be trained by VHS. Because VHS teachers are nearly always at locations remote from the students in their NetCourse, and because the students themselves are at multiple schools, the site coordinators play an important role in mediating among the participants.

Schools have selected different kinds of school employees to serve as site coordinators. About a third have been teachers, and a nearly equal proportion have been technology specialists. The remaining coordinators have been mostly administrators, media specialists, or guidance counselors.

The role of the site coordinator is a distinctive feature of the VHS structure and is important to its successful implementation; many other virtual schools either do not require an onsite coordinator in local schools or have only recently begun to emphasize this function. Because the position was novel, the coordinator's role was not detailed at the beginning of the project. As VHS was implemented at each founding school, this position and its functions became defined. In a majority of schools, these functions include:

- Promoting and marketing the VHS project within the school and recruiting and selecting students for the project
- Handling local administrative issues related to course credits, grades, and so on
- Distributing to students, and later collecting for reuse, any special materials the VHS teachers have assigned for online courses being taken by VHS students in this school, such as a textbook, other assigned readings not available online, or equipment
- Reporting to administrators or school board members on the status of the project
- Coordinating with VHS central staff
- Assisting students who have difficulties with technology
- Assisting VHS students, monitoring their work, and communicating with their VHS teachers

Some of these functions are administrative overhead for the project: promoting and marketing the VHS project, reporting to the school board, coordinating with VHS staff. These are important but relatively modest tasks that enable the project to work at a local site. Students' teachers normally would perform other parts of the job: monitoring students' progress and addressing problems with their work. In about half of the participating schools, all the VHS students do their work during the same period, whether in the site coordinator's classroom, the school media center, or a computer lab. In the schools that use this approach, the site coordinator can circulate among the students, assisting them with technical problems and monitoring their progress. In other schools, the site coordinator keeps track of VHS students who work in different locations at different times. In any case, the coordinators are expected to know what is required of students in their VHS courses and to maintain communications with the students' VHS teachers. One student volunteered that the site coordinator at her school was the "real teacher" in the VHS project.

The range of site coordinators' responsibilities was also reflected in the student survey fielded in the fall of 2000: 67% said that their coordinators handled administrative matters, such as grades for their VHS course; 59% said they communicated with their VHS teacher; 40% said they helped them stay on schedule and make progress in their course; and 33% said they helped them use LearningSpace and the computer. A majority of the students (73%) said they agreed (45%) or strongly agreed (28%) that they regularly communicated with their VHS site coordinator, and 88% agreed (41%) or strongly agreed (47%) that the site coordinator was regularly available for assistance.

VHS Central Staff

For the 5 years beginning in October 1996 and ending in the summer of 2001, the VHS central administration was based at the Concord Consortium and Hudson Public Schools, both located in Massachusetts, less than an hour's drive from Boston. Dr. Robert Tinker, president of the Concord Consortium, and Dr. Sheldon Berman, superintendent of the Hudson, Massachusetts, Public Schools, were the principal investigators for the VHS grant. However, Bruce Droste from the Concord Consortium and Elizabeth Pape from Hudson Public Schools had responsibility for the day-to-day management of the project and thus had the greatest interaction with the participating schools. Mr. Droste is a former high school principal; Ms. Pape has had experience in business and has served as a school district technology coordinator.

Beginning in the fall of 2001, VHS became an independent, nonprofit organization, based in Maynard, Massachusetts. As the school year began, Bruce Droste and Elizabeth Pape, who did most of the business planning leading to the transition, remained the key leaders of the school. Among the many responsibilities of these two individuals are managing the nationwide marketing of VHS; recruitment, selection, and preparation of schools; preparation of VHS teachers and site coordinators; and establishment of VHS policies to guide student selection, grading, and assignment of credits.

A staff of about eight other people is also part of the central VHS administration. These include technical services and support staff, instructors in the TLC and the NIM, and others. In addition, VHS employs a number of people part time to act as faculty advisors.

A list of all the responsibilities of the VHS staff would be lengthy. For example, VHS has developed methods for enrolling students and has established policies for allowing students to drop or add courses. Central staff members manage personnel problems (such as when a teacher has a long-term illness or a sudden emergency) and resolve disagreements about grading that may arise. Staff members routinely monitor online courses to make sure they are operating effectively.

Members of the central staff also supervise the work of faculty advisors. These advisors act somewhat in the role of department chairs and do in-depth examinations of courses, especially new ones, to be sure that they meet VHS's quality standards. In regular high schools, each department normally has a single chairperson. However, there are so many VHS courses in each discipline that multiple faculty advisors are required. VHS began to use faculty advisors as the number of courses grew too large for central staff members to keep close tabs on all of them.

Managing the technology itself is another responsibility of central staff. After operating VHS for several years, staff decided to outsource the maintenance of the servers. Nonetheless, if there are problems with the availability of the servers or other technological glitches, the central staff members are ultimately responsible.

Although no school administration is flawless, in discussions at case study schools and in survey comments regarding administrative operations, the VHS staff members were often praised for their willingness to work closely with participants at the schools to improve operations and for their efforts to resolve issues that confronted teachers and coordinators. One teacher commented, "The staff at VHS central was great. This was my first year, and I never would have made it without their help." In the fall 2000 survey, 84% of the students agreed or strongly agreed that "VHS Administration at Concord and Hudson has been responsive, if needed."

Technological Infrastructure

Although students taking VHS courses do not need any special software (other than a standard Web browser), LearningSpace is the software that is used to create and deliver NetCourses. The choice of LearningSpace was an early and important decision in the evolution of VHS. Developed and supported by Lotus Development Corp. (owned by IBM), the LearningSpace software was still under development when VHS decided to use it as a central element in designing and delivering courses. Lotus's headquarters in Cambridge, Massachusetts, are not far from Concord and Hudson, and VHS was able to work with the company, which upgraded LearningSpace in part to meet the needs of VHS. As a result of these changes, and for other reasons, technical difficulties in using LearningSpace diminished greatly in VHS's second year of operation (1998–1999). Participants reported that LearningSpace, in general, was much easier to use than the year before. Teachers reported greater efficiency in navigating the software and in managing the logistics of their courses. Nonetheless, it still takes time to learn to use LearningSpace, either as a student or, particularly, as a teacher (because the latter requires more technical know-how). VHS has added a Student Orientation module to the beginning of each VHS course, which is designed to familiarize students with the use of LearningSpace. In fall 2000, 86% of the students agreed (47%) or strongly agreed (39%) that they had gained enough knowledge in the Student Orientation to successfully navigate in their VHS course. (Additional detail about the structure of courses created with LearningSpace is provided in Chapter 3.)

Server problems in the first semester of the project were occasionally serious impediments, slowing down or even preventing access to the courses. That is seldom the case anymore. However, any time new technological components were added to VHS, there was a period of adjustment. That was the case for VHS as recently as during the 2000–2001 school year, when the central staff worked with an outside company to implement a new way for schools to enroll students through the Web. A series of unexpected problems slowed the enrollment process and frustrated many users. Overall, however, as new uses of technology have become routine, satisfaction with the performance of the technologies has been high. For example, a majority of the teachers in the fall of 2000 were "very satisfied" with the accessibility of the VHS servers, and only 5% were "not very" or "not at all" satisfied.

Evaluation Activities

Evaluation has been an important component of the Virtual High School from its inception. A preliminary evaluation plan was prepared by SRI International (http://www.sri.com/policy) and became part of the VHS proposal to the Challenge Grant program. Work on the evaluation began shortly after the VHS grant was awarded in October 1996. The primary goals of the evaluation were to document VHS activities, assess the impacts of the project, and identify lessons learned as a result of its implementation. In addition to providing an annual series of public reports about VHS (see http://www.sri.com/policy/ctl/html/vhs. html), the evaluation team also provided VHS staff with formative evaluation data to help them make midcourse operational changes.

The evaluation draws on multiple data sources, including surveys, case studies, interviews with consortium staff, and document reviews. Several special studies were conducted by the evaluation team, such as a comparison of face-to-face and online courses. An expert panel was convened by SRI in 1999 to develop standards for VHS courses and to assess the quality of a representative set of a dozen courses in a wide variety of disciplines.

The primary data sources for the evaluation are surveys of participants and case studies of selected schools. Over 5 years, SRI conducted more than 20 surveys, covering the experiences and opinions of VHS teachers and site coordinators, as well as school principals and district superintendents. SRI also helped VHS staff design surveys for students, which were administered online at the end of each semester.

From 1997 to 2001, site visits were conducted at nine schools, distributed across six states and including several regions of the United States. A variety of school types (e.g., urban and rural, more and less wealthy, etc.) were selected as case study sites. At each institution, SRI interviewed teachers who were teaching a NetCourse for students, the school's VHS coordinator, the school's principal, and others, as appropriate. The district superintendent for each school was often interviewed as well. In addition, focus group sessions were conducted with a number of students at the schools who were taking NetCourses offered by other participating schools.

It is unusual, if not unique, for an online school to commission such a wide variety of evaluation activities; the Florida Virtual School apparently is the only other virtual schooling program that has been systematically evaluated by an external evaluator (Bigbie & McCarroll, 2000). One result is that this book is able to draw on a very large set of data that provides accurate information about the evolution of VHS over 5 years.

One High School's Experiences with VHS

Although statistical data can provide an accurate picture of the responses of large populations, case studies often add details and provide insights that are as important as so-called hard data in understanding social phenomena. Westborough High School, located in Westborough, Massachusetts, is one of the schools visited by the evaluators over several different years. This section briefly describes some of Westborough's experiences with the Virtual High School.

Westborough is a prosperous suburban town located about 30 miles west of Boston near Route 495. The school district of about 3,000 students reflects a growing and increasingly cosmopolitan community with an interest in education. Nearly 90% of the district's students are White, compared with a state average of fewer than 80%.

The school was one of the "founding schools," meaning that it has been part of VHS since 1996. The district's superintendent told the evaluators he first supported participation in VHS in part because he was looking for a program that would help "move the school into the 21st century." The principal of the high school shared the superintendent's enthusiasm for VHS. As of the 2001–2002 school year, the school continues to participate in the consortium.

During the summer of 1997, two of Westborough's teachers were trained in the TLC. Tracy Reynolds (now Tracy Sheehan) designed The Bioethics Symposium. David Jost designed Music Appreciation and Composition. Ms. Sheehan found the TLC long, hard work, but very useful. She was determined to master the technology and to put together all the Bioethics assignments before first teaching the course online, and was able to accomplish both those things. Mr. Jost also found many of the VHS staff helpful and thought the TLC was useful. However, he noted that it was far easier to stimulate online discussion among a group of teachers in the TLC than to stimulate discussion among students taking virtual courses. Ms. Sheehan agreed.

Both teachers first offered their VHS courses in the fall of the 1997–1998 school year. Because the courses were one-semester electives (as is the case for most VHS courses), each was offered twice, once in the fall semester and again in the spring.

Bioethics

Ms. Sheehan did undergraduate and graduate work at Boston University, focusing on education and biology. She has taught at the junior high, high school, and college levels. At the time she signed up to work with VHS, Ms. Sheehan was in her fifth year as a teacher. "It sounded exciting," she said of VHS. "The science department chair approached and asked if I'd like to do it. Though I thought that maybe a more experienced teacher should do it, I jumped on it."

Unlike many VHS courses, which are designed especially for VHS, Ms. Sheehan and the science department chair developed the Bioethics course and first taught it face to face in the fall of 1996. During 1997–1998, Ms. Sheehan taught both virtual and in-person sections of Bioethics, and she has continued to teach the online course since that time. More information about the Bioethics course is provided in Chapter 3.

Music Appreciation and Composition

At the time he began the TLC, Mr. Jost had been teaching for 17 years, including 14 in Westborough. He has taught at the elementary, middle, and high school levels. Mr. Jost has a master's degree in music, and when he began with

VHS he was actively performing on both the saxophone and the clarinet. In addition to playing professionally, he was teaching a wide variety of courses at the high school, including a combination course called Modernism: Music, English, and Art of the Early 20th Century. His involvement with VHS began when the principal called him to her office and said, "I have something I want you to think about." One of the motivating factors for him was that he had had a bout with a serious illness 10 years earlier and missed students a lot. "The idea of a virtual school was one motivator for me to participate," he said.

The Music Appreciation and Composition course is one of the more challenging courses to teach online. Students were provided with a set of music CDs, and, in addition, the course relied on computer music files in the "MIDI" format. Each student was also provided with a computer program called Music Shop, which allows sound files to be played through a computer or composed, using a computer mouse for input, and stored in the MIDI format. By the second year, Mr. Jost estimated that he was spending about 15 hours per week teaching the virtual course. Despite the long hours required, Mr. Jost remained "fascinated by VHS." He believes that virtual courses are a way to reach students who otherwise would not be able to participate, such as homebound students.

VHS Students at the School

Almost all the students at Westborough High School who have participated in VHS have been juniors or seniors. During the 1998–1999 school year, Westborough accumulated nearly 60 VHS credits, earned by more than 40 different students. Some students enrolled for courses both semesters, and others enrolled for only one semester. The students were involved in many different VHS courses—but, as is the norm in all the VHS schools, none of the Westborough students enrolled in either of the VHS courses taught by teachers at their own school.

Most of the students' comments offered to the evaluators about VHS were positive. Students were attracted both by the opportunity to enroll in courses that otherwise would not have been available to them and by the flexibility of scheduling their own time. One student said:

> I wanted to try a virtual course. . . . But I couldn't type very well,
> and I didn't know that much about computers. I don't have a com-
> puter at home, either. . . . The course definitely met my expectations.
> . . . And it did help me with computer skills.

Students agreed that the school's VHS site coordinator, Paul Vital, did an excellent job. As the school's computer teacher, Mr. Vital was well equipped to provide help with computers and the LearningSpace Web interface. Many of the students used Mr. Vital's computer lab as the place where they did most of their VHS work. Some also worked on VHS courses from home, which is the norm; in the 2000–2001 school year, more than 80% of all VHS students reported working from home at least some of the time.

Summary of Westborough's Experiences

From the Westborough district superintendent to the students themselves, there has been a lot of enthusiasm for the Virtual High School. The participants were patient with the first-year start-up problems, understanding that they were inevitable and that it would take some time for such problems to be solved. The superintendent felt that the district's involvement with VHS would have beneficial impacts on *all* students, not just those taking virtual courses, and there is evidence to that effect. For example, one VHS teacher reported: "I've changed. I'm using technology more in my regular courses. . . . Plus, I'm helping my colleagues." Community support for VHS has remained strong, as has support from the school board.

This is not to say that the teachers or students always think that participating in VHS is easy. One teacher said, "It's like you are a first-year teacher all over again." There is much for all the participants to learn in order to make the virtual courses effective and smooth-running. Students, who often have strong opinions about *all* their teachers, seem to believe that the style of the teacher is even more critical to the success of VHS courses than it is for regular high school courses.

Over the years, many recommendations for improving VHS have emerged from people at Westborough. For example, one recommendation was that the VHS staff ought to develop a unit or module for students about how to use the LearningSpace technology and that this unit might be included as part of each virtual course. This recommendation was implemented beginning with the second semester that VHS courses were offered. (VHS students' high comfort level with the technology after using this module is documented through the surveys, as noted earlier.) The roles of VHS staff in maintaining the quality of the courses and in performing central administrative functions were other areas in which suggestions were made, and many of these suggestions have been incorporated into VHS policies and procedures.

Westborough High School's enthusiasm for VHS is demonstrated by its participation for many years. Beginning in the 2001–2002 school year, Westborough, like all the participating schools, has had to pay to continue to be a member of the consortium. Although the federal grant initially paid for some schools to join VHS, the transition of VHS to independent, nonprofit status and the end of the federal grant means that VHS must now meet the demands of the marketplace to survive.

Comparisons of VHS with Other Online Schools

VHS is just one model for providing courses online. The nature of this model can be understood in part according to its goals. VHS's primary goal was to establish a nonprofit national membership consortium to share resources. Under this model, participating schools nationwide both contribute to and benefit from the online course catalog. Some of the other providers of online courses that are aimed at high school students, such as Apex and Intelligent Education, Inc. (IEI), are also national in scope, like VHS. Most of these national providers are for-profit entities, whereas VHS is a nonprofit.

However, most online schools—such as Alabama Online High School, Kentucky Virtual High School, New Mexico Virtual School, and Houston Independent School District Virtual School, and many more, including others that were identified in Chapter 1—have emerged in recent years from more local goals. These schools sought to provide an electronic course option to their students that would support equitable access to high-quality teaching while meeting local and state standards, as well as to offer flexible learning choices for students with different learning styles. Their programs have followed a different model of development from VHS. Usually, either a state or regional entity developed the courses and infrastructure in-house, or they contracted with for-profit companies to supplement their in-house development process.

For most national and local course providers, apart from VHS, the involvement of teachers in a new teaching approach has been a secondary goal. However, this goal appears to be gaining prominence as online schools grapple with the challenge of enlarging their catalogs while maintaining quality in online courses.

In addition to the providers whose service is primarily to offer national and local netcourses, another type of company is important in the emerging market for online high school courses. These companies, such as Blackboard and eCollege/eClassroom, provide tools and services that others use to create their own virtual courses. Blackboard, for example, markets services to individual schools and districts that allow teachers either to supplement face-to-face courses with an organized set of online resources or to create entire online courses. The services that are provided by such companies include software tools supporting enrollment, grading, course delivery, and chat rooms, among others.

Understanding the array of entities that are springing up is made more complicated by the fact that online providers may fall into more than one of these categories. For example, Apex offers courses nationwide and also markets tools and services that others can use to create or support their own courses. Virtual high schools in New Mexico, Michigan, and Kentucky, among others, use Apex, but they have their own identities and goals. eCollege also claims to have the Kentucky Virtual High School as a customer.

Course Offerings

The number of courses offered by the different providers varies greatly. Some programs, such as IEI and Florida Virtual School, offer a large number of courses that are core to the high school curriculum. For example, among the 98 courses offered by IEI are courses such as Language Arts and American Literature, Algebra 1 and 2, Biology, and World History. Indeed, students can earn a college preparatory high school diploma from IEI totally online. On the other hand, some programs offer a rather narrow range of courses. For example, Apex currently offers only 16 courses—10 advanced placement (AP) and 6 foreign-language courses. VHS is unique in offering a large number—more than 120—of specialized, often elective courses. Unlike courses at IEI or Florida Virtual School, VHS courses do not compete with the standard courses offered by most schools. Rather, as administrators, teachers, and students point out, these are courses that would not be offered otherwise by participating schools.

Some of the providers have carved out content niches, such as AP courses in the case of Apex Learning. Yet this business approach appears to be shifting, with most commercial providers now seeking to offer a broader selection of course types. "AP has been a great place to get this industry started. Our student numbers and commitment numbers are quite a bit larger than everybody else. We have 23 state-level contracts [and this number is growing]," said Keith Oelrich, CEO of Apex Learning of Bellevue, Washington, in a 2001 interview. "But the downside is, we're appropriate for such a small percentage of the total student population. So you don't get a lot of 'mindshare' of the total student and parent population."

What courses get offered by an online provider is a complex question. Providers may limit offerings to those that they have developed, or they may have a larger menu of courses produced by several different providers. For example, CyberSchool and Florida Virtual School both function like VHS in that they offer only courses that their member teachers design. In contrast, New Mexico's virtual school has designed its school's Web page as a gateway to a variety of national providers' programs and services, offering everything from AP course catalogs to core course catalogs to online test preparation. Kentucky's virtual school presents a single school course catalog, designed primarily by one national for-profit provider, but features a localized interface, including the state seal and descriptions of how state educators have reviewed and approved the online courses.

As has been noted already, a number of for-profit providers, such as class.com and eClassroom, eCollege's new K–12 division, help districts build course catalogs. They provide access to existing online courses and provide technical support to help local districts create their own courses. "We take their content and build it into a course," said Justin McMorrow, eClassroom's general manager of K–12 education. Often, districts begin with ambitious plans to put many of their own courses online, then scale back and provide a mixed offering of custom-designed courses and courses created by others, such as those from IEI, which provides a broad selection of courses and a teaching staff.

The class.com program has also found that districts seek to customize the courses that it has developed over the past several years. "We do have good content, but what we find is, because every school district needs to meet their own local standards, we need to provide a vehicle to take our content and customize it," said Katherine Endacott, class.com's president, CEO, and chairman of the board. To support such customization, class.com has associated with infrastructure providers, such as Blackboard Inc. in Washington, D.C., which provide tools that allow teachers to convert word-processed course documents into Web documents in a few easy steps.

Although many states are setting up virtual schools, in most states these are at an early stage of development and the course catalogs are still evolving. Alabama Online High School, for example, began with a focus on core courses to improve educational equity across the state's rural schools. Today, the school is moving toward offering more advanced electives and courses, too. "It's amazing. We keep talking about potential. We have 25 courses that will be up by January 1, 2002," said Robert Youngblood, administrator of Alabama Online High School. "Once we start getting our electives, that's where everybody sees this. Small schools see this as core courses. Big schools, they want electives and they're willing to pay for those. We're having a lot of gifted students and college-bound students wanting to learn this way."

Cost and Tuition Arrangements

Virtual schools vary considerably in the tuition that they charge for their courses each semester. They also vary somewhat in who pays these costs. For example, IEI markets directly to students, and the students pay tuition when they enroll in a course. In 2001, IEI tuition ranged from $250 for a parent-directed course to $500 for an honors course with instructor support. Other programs market to the school districts or schools but charge the institution a per-student enrollment fee. For example, Apex charges a school or district $450 for each student who enrolls in one of its instructor-led courses. Similarly, CyberSchool charges schools from $300 to $350 (depending on the number of enrollments) for each student enrolled in one of its courses. CyberSchool, in turn, distributes 85% of this tuition back to the school that is offering the course. The VHS model is unique in that it does not charge tuition per se; instead, schools pay a participation fee.

Both not-for-profit and for-profit course content providers develop affiliation or licensing agreements with states, school districts, or schools that are seeking to offer online courses to their students. These agreements usually require a subsidy of some or all of the students' course costs. Until the 2001–2002 school year, VHS involved schools free of charge in its program, using the federal grant, but as it moved to become a self-supporting not-for-profit program, it needed to depend increasingly on membership fees from schools. In some cases, states, districts, and schools have been able to turn to state legislatures to offset both start-up and ongoing tuition expenses for in-state students, while charging full price to out-of-state students. For example, the Florida Virtual School receives more than $6 million annually from the state and does not charge fees to the state's public schools or home schoolers.

In a few cases, districts must bear the costs of home-schooled students who enroll in online charter schools. Pennsylvania state law supports this option, for example. (See Chapter 6 for more information on this topic.)

Role of Teachers

Virtual schools differ in the role teachers play in designing and offering their courses. For many, such as Apex, IEI, class.com, and Florida Virtual School (FVS), the courses are designed by different people than those who teach them. In some, the students are engaged primarily in self-study, and the instructors grade assignments and are available to respond to students' questions and needs. This is the case for IEI and class.com. In some programs, such as Apex and FVS, teachers take a more active role in directing the course and monitoring students, even if they did not design the course themselves.

Only in VHS and CyberSchool are the courses typically taught by the same instructor who developed them. Much like classes in the face-to-face world, teachers in these courses are responsible not only for the course material but for how the course progresses, what activities the students are engaged in, and how the students are doing in their courses.

Supporting Teachers

VHS's online learning courses for teachers, the TLC and the NIM, remain relatively unusual. In light of VHS's consortium approach, providing such teacher training online is a vital component of the model. CyberSchool also offers individual teachers a fee-based online course designed to help them create online courses. In addition to supporting teachers designing online courses, in recent years VHS also has been educating other teachers online to teach sections of already-created courses.

Several of the for-profit content providers, such as Apex Learning, eClassroom, and class.com, offer contracting districts face-to-face professional development workshops to help district teachers either design their own courses or teach already-created courses. Some for-profit online high school providers, such as class.com, are also developing online professional development communities to provide continuing support for online teachers. "We will have the largest body of knowledge in secondary schools. We will know what is working and what's not. We'll be hooking all those teachers together with teacher-to-teacher communication," said CEO Katherine Endacott. "As we launch our user groups, we're getting a critical mass of teachers. We have 300 teachers trained now. Some are in urban areas and some in rural. It's going to be a wonderful way for them to learn from each other." Similarly, VHS has provided a place online for its teachers to have threaded discussions, known as "the water cooler," which provides a form of ongoing professional support.

Supporting Students

VHS's years of experience with site coordinators and the program's commitment to professional development for site coordinators are also unusual. Several other providers of online courses said they were discovering the importance of local mentors. In New Mexico, for example, state virtual-school organizers designed their own local site coordinator training program because they found that this important role baffled many educators. The developer of the site coordinator training program, Steven Sanchez, director of curriculum, instruction, and learning technologies at the New Mexico Department of Education, said that many site coordinators felt that "the kids were pretty much in charge of their learning; they were interacting with a teacher. What's my functional role?" The state needed to step in and provide assistance.

Different commercial course providers have different requirements for adults to provide on-site student support. For example, in IEI's parent-directed courses, a parent mentors the student's independent study. Apex encourages on-site mentors at the participating schools to support the students. As mentioned above, VHS requires schools to provide a site coordinator for this purpose. More and more providers are strongly encouraging or requiring districts to provide this type of help. "I think the place where we have to be careful is making sure that we get the support at the building level of the principals, the faculty, and the guidance counselors," said Keith Oelrich, CEO of Apex Learning. "What we want to make sure is these students are not off to the side somewhere because they're taking courses online." Sometimes the requirement for on-site mentor training comes from the school district itself.

Enrolling Students

Enrolling students is another issue that gets handled differently by different providers. Under its national membership model, VHS bundles student enrollments into blocks of 20 students or 10 students per school, with these students then enrolling in the VHS courses of their choice on a first-come, first-served basis. This "blocked" enrollment approach is unique to VHS.

In a few cases, such as IEI, students can enroll directly with a provider of online courses, without the need to work through a local school or district. Other online course providers, such as Apex Learning and CyberSchool, establish enrollment expectations and prices with contracting states, districts, and schools during licensing negotiations, and then students can enroll directly with the applicable school district or online school (e.g., Kentucky's) on a first-come, first-served basis.

The local school district often assumes a major responsibility for student outreach and recruitment. In these cases, the national provider—VHS, Apex, CyberSchool, or some other one—provides courses but is not primarily responsible for recruiting students.

Course Credit and Course Accreditation

Under virtually all of these approaches, participating schools are required to grant students credit and grades for the virtual courses. Among the national virtual-school offerings, only IEI provides a diploma directly to the participating students. With other programs, such as class.com, CyberSchool, Apex, and VHS, the course credit is offered by the participating school district.

Often, national virtual-schooling programs rely on their participating school district customers to provide accreditation within their states for the courses taken by their students, if accreditation is necessary. The programs offered by IEI are accredited by the Accrediting Commission for Independent Study. A few programs are themselves accredited by some outside agency. For example, CyberSchool is accredited by the Northwest Association of Schools and Colleges, the Commission on International and Trans-Regional Accreditation, and the Accreditation Commission for International Internet Education. The class.com courses were developed as part of the high school curriculum of the University of Nebraska's Independent Study High School, which is accredited by the State of Nebraska and the North Central Association of Colleges and Schools.

Summary and Conclusions

With its inception in 1996, the Virtual High School has constructed a distinctive model for offering high-quality, specialized courses on the Internet. The model includes a consortium of schools, whose high-quality teachers design and offer a wide range of courses in return for slots in these courses for their own students. VHS students are supported by both the VHS NetCourse teachers and local site coordinators. Both of these sets of participants engage in extensive online training to prepare for their new roles. The VHS central staff provide teachers, coordinators, and students with a variety of services that support their efforts. The success of this model is evidenced by the fact that nearly 200 schools participated, more than 120 NetCourses were offered, and there were more than 7,000 student semester enrollments in VHS over the first 4 years of operation. Administrators, teachers, and students agree that through their participation in VHS, they have access to courses that otherwise would not be available to them.

As more and more national, state, and local providers have begun offering online courses, schools, districts, and states are faced with a wide variety of options. Some course providers operate nationally, but many operate at a regional, state, or local level. Some companies provide tools to help schools create their own online courses. There are both for-profit and nonprofit course providers.

These providers' structures and their methods of operation are also diverse. Those interested in understanding the options that they face in choosing among the providers need to be aware of such key factors as the types of courses that are offered, the source and role of the teachers, how credit is awarded, and whether or not a local coordinator is recommended or required. In almost all cases, the responsibility for recruiting students lies with the local school or district. A good source of information about what to look for in online courses is an article by Berman and Pape (2001), titled "A Consumer's Guide to Online Courses."

VHS stands out as a singular pioneering effort, both for its structure and for its mission. Its consortium approach permits VHS to marshal the creativity of a talented group of high school teachers throughout the nation to create a broad, electives-oriented course catalog. VHS also has developed an extensive program of online pedagogy for both teachers and site coordinators.

As one of the earliest online schools, VHS has been highly visible and has been observed by other virtual schools. Three different innovations—the broad catalog focusing especially on electives, a required online teacher professional development course, and the use of trained site coordinators—have more recently emerged among a number of the other virtual high schools. VHS's experience in these areas makes it a model for others to study, and many have done so. As more high school courses are offered online, it appears likely that there will be a growing demand for a broad range of netcourses, professional development to help more teachers use the Internet, and effective site monitoring.

However, as distinctive as VHS is, it shares with other online programs many features that replicate the "standard school grammar." Although technology promised to bring significant changes to education, many of the features of virtual school programs are strikingly familiar. Like most bricks-and-mortar schools, VHS has a central administration, a set of courses, a standard calendar, teachers, students, grades, and credit hours. All of these make it easier for VHS to fit into the structure of the school and, no doubt, contribute to its success.

But what of the VHS experience from the inside? What is it like to teach or take a VHS NetCourse online? Is that where fundamental changes in schooling are taking place? It is to these questions that we turn next.

Chapter 3

THE VHS EXPERIENCE

Many of the virtual schooling pioneers, including Bob Tinker and Shelley Berman, were initially inspired by the potential of technology to foster educational change and improvement. Tinker and Berman felt that technology could be used to support significant educational reform. They believed that netcourses could bring the world into schools by tapping the knowledge and experience of corporations, universities, and individuals anywhere. These resources could be used to accelerate students' advanced study in specialized courses. The Internet also could take the schools into the real world; these resources could be used to integrate students into work and society by providing them with academic support as they made their transition. Finally, they believed that netcourses could be used for teacher professional development, aiding teachers at a distance to learn new content and adapt their teaching strategies to take advantage of the new medium.

Similarly, the founders of the Florida Virtual School were convinced that the development of the Internet offered a unique opportunity to combine the best technology with the best instructional practices to provide students with educational choice and equal access to standards-based courses that otherwise might not be available. They believed that online learning could provide a rich collaborative and active environment where students could learn at their own pace and share experiences with peers and mentors.

The technology-based visions of other virtual-schooling pioneers are no less grand, although educational change is not their focus. The mission statement of Intelligent Education, Inc. (IEI) is to "use advanced technology to provide universal access to outstanding programs in a cost-effective manner" (http://www.intelligented.com). Apex Learning's stated vision is to "create a world where every student, in every school, has access to every class desired" (http://www.apexlearning.com).

It is clear that technology is playing a crucial role for the Virtual High School and other virtual schools. These programs are using the Internet to offer courses that otherwise would not be available to thousands of students. But beyond delivering courses at a distance, how is technology being used to create the virtual-school experience? How does technology shape what teachers and students do in virtual courses? Does it live up to the promises cited by its proponents? How similar or different are virtual courses from those that meet face to face? Is technology successfully used to transform education?

We already demonstrated in Chapter 2 that VHS and other virtual schools are similar in structure to bricks-and-mortar schools. As do "real" schools, vir-

tual schools have course catalogs and credit hours, admissions and grading policies, administrators and schedules, and, of course, teachers and students. All these
components make it easier for schools, teachers, and students to adopt these
virtual programs and fit them into the current school structure. But an important
question is: Once you walk into the virtual classroom, how does the experience
of schooling change? In this chapter, the nature of VHS courses is described in
detail. We look at the way this experience is shaped by the technological environment used to deliver the VHS courses and similar environments in other
virtual programs. We examine the technology from the perspective of a sample
VHS course—the Bioethics Symposium. We discuss VHS teachers' experiences
in designing and teaching their courses and VHS students' experiences in taking
these courses. We feature a comparative study in which we examine the experiences of students and teachers in courses taught both face to face and virtually.
Finally, we identify and examine the characteristics that make an online course
outstanding.

The LearningSpace Environment and
an Exemplary VHS NetCourse

The work of teachers and students in the Virtual High School is very much
framed by the software environment that is used: IBM's Lotus LearningSpace.
Teachers develop and administer their courses within this environment, which
sits on top of a relational database that stores assignments, course discussions,
and student records. Students enter their courses by using a standard Web
browser, such as Netscape Navigator or Internet Explorer.

Once inside LearningSpace, as implemented in VHS, students see many
components and features that are similar to those in the traditional school classroom. At the highest level of structure, LearningSpace has four components (see
Figure 3.1): the Schedule, the MediaCenter, the CourseRoom, and Profiles. Each

Figure 3.1

Schedule   MediaCenter   CourseRoom   Profiles

of these corresponds to a significant component of the real-world classroom. The Schedule has many of the features of the typical course syllabus. The MediaCenter is where course materials are stored, much like the school library or media center. The CourseRoom is where the classroom action occurs, specifically, asynchronous discussions between the teacher and students in the course. And the Profiles provide students with information on their teacher and other students in the course, information that students in a real school might pick up in casual conversation.

The software environments for other virtual schools have corresponding functions. For example, the environment used by the Florida Virtual School has Orientation, Profiles, Assignments, My Files, Discussion, Chat, Announcements, Glossary, and an e-global Library. The Apex Learning environment has a Class Center with areas called The Basics (i.e., orientation), Syllabus, My Work, Announcements, and Discussions. The Syllabus contains assignments and resource materials, such as tutorials and exercises.

The Bioethics Symposium

Let us see how the LearningSpace environment is implemented and used in a sample VHS course. We have selected the Bioethics Symposium, offered by Tracy Sheehan at Westborough High School in Westborough, Massachusetts. As mentioned in Chapter 2, Tracy Sheehan did her undergraduate and graduate work at Boston University. At the time of this writing, she has been teaching for 11 years, 5 online with VHS. She has taught courses in science at the junior high school, high school, and college levels. She has also mentored other teachers in teaching online for VHS as part of their Teachers Learning Conference (TLC) training. She has taught the Bioethics course face to face for 6 years and through VHS for 5.

We use Bioethics as an example because it was one of our case study courses for 2 years and because it was one of the courses examined by our expert panel, convened to develop and apply standards to assess VHS courses. The expert panel rated as "high quality" more than half of the courses that it studied, including this one. In fact, the Bioethics Symposium is one of the more outstanding courses that VHS offers, according to the panel. But we will supplement the experience reported here with survey data from large numbers of VHS teachers and observations from other case study courses, such as Poetry and Poetics for Publication, taught by Anita Bergh at Kennedy High School in Fremont, California; Russian, Soviet, and Post-Soviet Studies, taught by Terry Haugen at Miramonte High School in Orinda, California; and Explorando varios aspectos de culturas hispanas a través del Internet (Exploring Various Aspects of Spanish Cultures Through the Internet), taught by Cynthia Costilla at Allen High School in Allen, Texas.

According to the VHS course catalog, the Bioethics Symposium is built around student inquiry and critical thinking. The course develops the concept of ethical decision making and how it applies to the increasing number of biology-related ethical decisions that students will have to make in the future. Students are told that they will investigate important ethical dilemmas from the past and that they will work in teams to investigate the social and scientific aspects of a particular question of their choosing, culminating in a multimedia presentation. How does this happen in a virtual course?

Students' Introduction to Bioethics Online

Students first meet Tracy Sheehan and other students in the course in the Profiles page for the Bioethics course (see Figure 3.2). They see a photo of the instructor and those of the others in the course, if the teacher and students chose to provide them. (Some teachers believe that one advantage of the online environment is not being able to form quick judgments of people by their appearance, and so it is common in VHS NetCourses not to see photos of the participants.) In addition, participants are able to read a short personal description that each student may have supplied.

Their introduction to the course content is through the Schedule (see Figure 3.3). Like a course syllabus, students get a week-by-week description of what the course will cover. Unlike a course syllabus, the various items are interconnected, or "hyperlinked," with the documents that reside elsewhere in the course environment. For example, the students may see that in week 5 they have a teacher's overview of the goals for the week. They may have several reading assignments and a writing assignment. The different kinds of entries are each signified by special icons. In Figure 3.3, we see that the topics for weeks 3 and 4 of Bioethics are Ethical Decision Making and Ethical Systems. In week 5, the topic is Reproductive Technology, and students have 10 reading, discussion, and writing assignments. Clicking on the fifth link in week 5 would take the student to the reading assignment displayed in Figure 3.4.

Alternatively, they could go to the MediaCenter (see Figure 3.5), which lists the various multimedia materials that the teacher has selected as course resources. These may be digital texts or hyperlinks to Web sites that the teacher may want the students to visit. Again, clicking on the links will immediately take the students to these resources. In Figure 3.5, we see that Tracy Sheehan has listed various book excerpts, news articles, and Web resources.

All the Bioethics materials we have seen so far were designed by Tracy Sheehan before the course went online. Many of them were developed during her TLC experience and were tuned and modified subsequently. This kind of planning is essential for a virtual course; this is not a place for teachers who merely keep one step ahead of their students.

Figure 3.2. Teacher's Profile, Bioethics Course

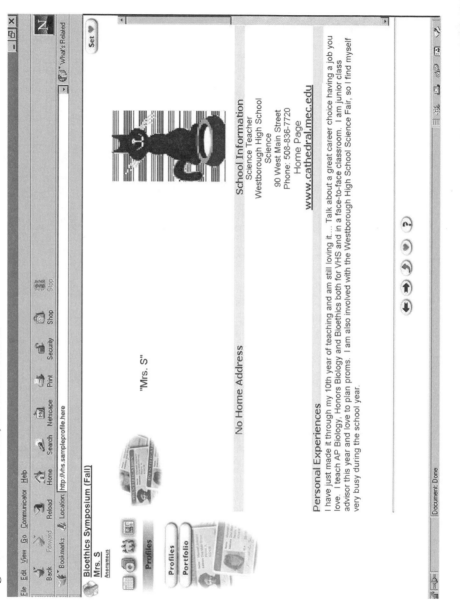

Figure 3.3. Schedule for Bioethics

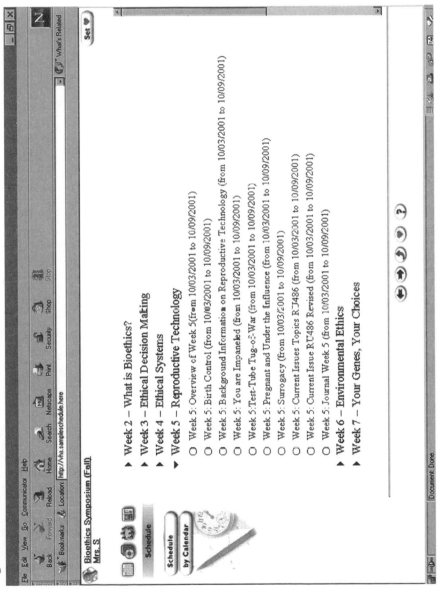

Figure 3.4. Reading Assignment for Bioethics

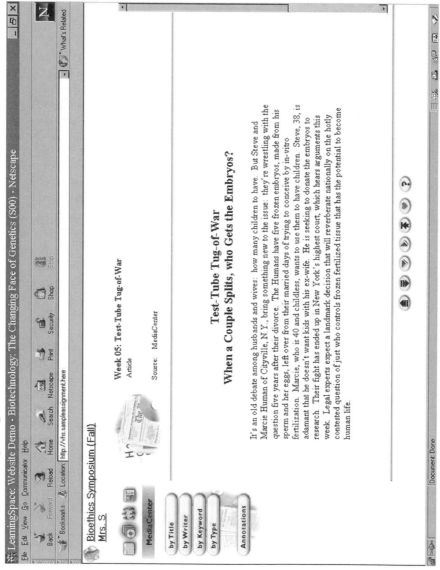

Figure 3.5. Media Center for Bioethics

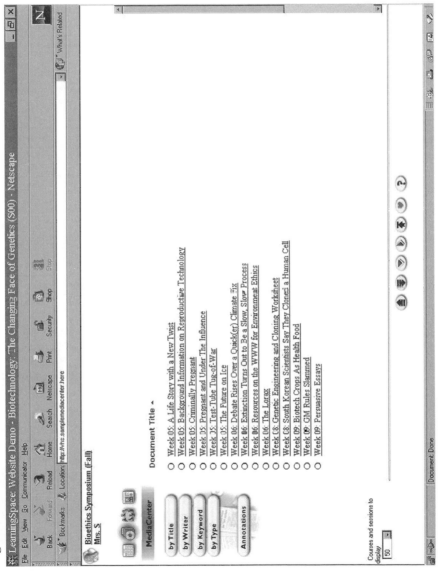

Figure 3.6. Assignment for Bioethics

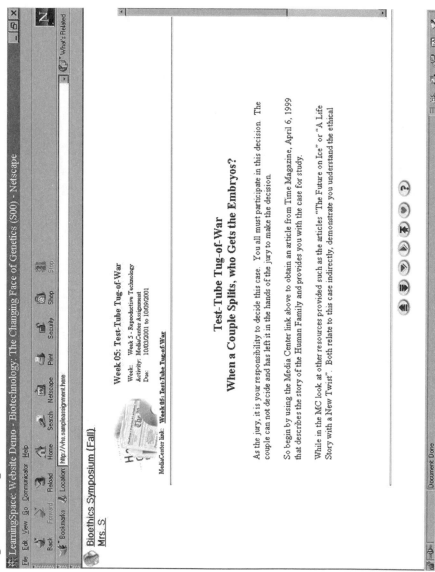

Figure 3.7. Course Room Discussion for Bioethics

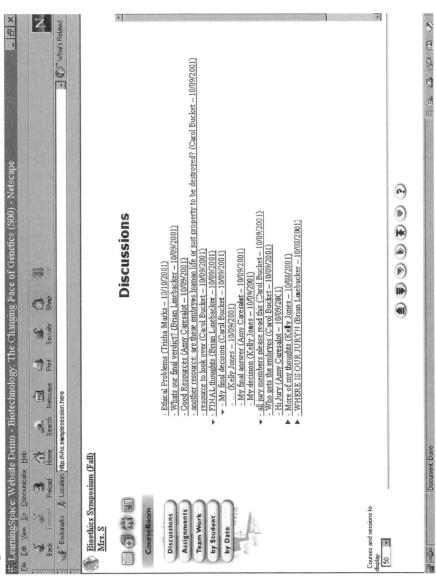

Participating Online

However, once the course has been designed and the materials organized, the stage has been set for learning. Much of this takes place in the CourseRoom, the place where students and teachers engage in threaded, asynchronous discussions. In Figure 3.6, we see that for week 5, Tracy Sheehan posted an assignment for students to participate in a jury deliberation and decision on an issue related to the topic for the week. In Figure 3.7, we see a portion of the students' deliberations. On October 9, 2001, Brian posted his final thoughts on the topic. Carol responded to this posting (as did Amy and Kelly), and Kelly replied to Carol's response.

What is novel about what we see here? We see hyperlinks to documents and URLs. In other courses, we might also see sound or movie files. The students' deliberations are preserved for further review and contemplation. However, there is nothing transformational about this environment. The software incorporates many of the standard features of a traditional classroom: teachers, other students, readings, assignments, grades, discussions—everything, perhaps, but lectures. In developing LearningSpace, the designers followed Donald Norman's (1988) basic precepts for helping users shift from an old environment to a new one: Familiar features from the old situation will help users understand the functions of a new technology environment. But in doing so, there is little in LearningSpace that is pedagogically innovative.

Nonetheless, what Tracy Sheehan and other VHS teachers did was to take these basic features and build interesting and effective courses for their online students. With regard to the Bioethics course, in summarizing his lengthy review, one of our expert panel members commented, "I found this to be a solid course, thoughtfully conceptualized and well designed in its features." The summary of the other panel member reviewing the course said, "Overall, this is an excellent course. . . . Congratulations on a job well done."

Activities in Bioethics

We can see how Tracy Sheehan designed such an exemplary course as we follow this experience through the semester. During the first week of the course, she presents the course syllabus and the requirements and grading standards of the course, and she teaches students how to move through the various parts of the Web site. The second week focuses on what bioethics is and the great breadth of the subject. Students are asked to go to the CourseRoom and post their own definitions of *bioethics* and those of four individuals they have interviewed. In addition, they are asked to find and post an article that they believe relates to bioethics. All students are to read all definitions and articles and comment on them. According to Sheehan, these initial discussions tend to be quite lively and generate a great deal of interest on students' part, setting the tone for the rest of the course. At the end of the week, she posts a reading that provides an authoritative definition of bioethics.

Week 2 also introduces the concept of a "case study." By the end of the week, students make their first entries in their course journals. Although the content of the entries is not graded, weekly journal entries are a course requirement. Their primary purpose is to provide a vehicle for students to take time to reflect about both the substance and form of the course. In addition, the instructor uses the journal writings to make adjustments to the course and to learn which students need extra help.

Equally important to the organizational and academic activities of the first two weeks are a series of activities that are intended to build community. Students are asked to describe their academic backgrounds and other information about themselves. As students read about one another, informal discussions among them begin in a section of the CourseRoom reserved for this purpose. Sheehan feels that these community-building activities are crucial to the success of the course, particularly in light of the controversial nature of some topics covered later in the course.

During week 5, students begin their consideration of the bioethics of various science topics. This consideration starts with reproductive technology and goes on to include biotechnology, medical ethics, and biotechnology in the courtroom. The format varies from week to week. In week 5, students are divided into groups of 10, each a "jury" that is assigned a case to study and about which they are to reach a consensus decision. Examples of case studies for reproductive-technology juries are: A divorcing couple has frozen embryos—to whom do they belong? Or does a woman have the right to drink while pregnant? Which is paramount: the right of the fetus or the right of the woman? In other weeks, the format may differ. For example, in week 6, the students write persuasive essays. In week 7, Biotechnology, they are paired as couples looking to undergo embryo screening, and they decide, as couples, what diseases they want their embryos screened for. In week 12, Medical Ethics, they role-play a medical board as a group of five that has to deal with rationing of medical care to patients. Each week, then, they express what they learn through readings and Web searches in a variety of ways. (Importantly, the expert panel reviewers both rated Bioethics as "exemplary" in the way that the teacher handled controversial issues—that is, not confusing fact, theory, and opinion, and not discouraging students from expressing alternative viewpoints.)

Another highlight of the week is Current Events. This weekly assignment gives the students the opportunity to bring an article to class about a current event dealing with bioethics. Students post a synopsis of each article and participate in a discussion about the articles.

Reaching a consensus decision on a topic typically requires a great deal of discussion among students. Most students like to get into these discussions early so that they can express their opinions before another student has had a chance to express the same opinion first and they are left without a meaningful comment. At the outset of the course, students have been informed that *meaningful* participation in discussions is a large part of their grade. Starting with early discussions and continuing over the duration of the course, the teacher makes it known that she is continually reading students' entries, although she does not post comments herself unless she sees serious misunderstandings, errors, or problems.

The fact that the discussions are asynchronous makes them more difficult than they would be in a classroom, but, according to the teacher, a week is usually long enough for all students to participate. Inevitably, some students participate less than others. Reticent students are often encouraged to participate by others in their group. Tracy also communicates with these students individually and gives them additional advice and direction.

During the last 3 weeks of the course, students create a symposium. Each student prepares a presentation discussing both sides of a biological issue, choosing from nine topics, which range from very science oriented (e.g., biotechnology) to more society oriented (e.g., drugs and sports). Presentations are prepared incrementally: First a topic is chosen, next a personal position statement is written, next background sources are found, and so on. At each stage, work is submitted to the teacher, who provides feedback. The final presentation can be in any Web-based form, such as a new Web site or a PowerPoint presentation.

According to Sheehan, there are disadvantages and advantages to the virtual teaching approach. Engaging students in teamwork, for example, is more difficult to achieve in the virtual course. However, an advantage is that it seems *easier* for some students in the virtual course to be frank in expressing their views about controversial issues, because typically they don't know the other students—a fact that, ironically, can lead to a *greater* sense of personal security.

The Experience in Other VHS NetCourses

Much of the success of Bioethics and many other VHS courses is due to the significant effort and creativity that VHS teachers bring to their courses. In our case study interviews with VHS teachers, they often told us that designing and teaching a virtual course took a lot of time and care. This was particularly so in the beginning, as teachers encountered the new challenges of virtual schooling. As one teacher put it, "It's like you are a first-year teacher all over again."

Time Needed by Teachers

This level of commitment and effort was sometimes motivated by the opportunity to be involved in an innovative new program, to "learn new things," or to use a new technology. But most often it was generated by the opportunity to teach a course that would not have been possible to teach otherwise. This was the primary reason for participating in VHS cited by teachers in our surveys. For example, Anita Bergh was an English teacher at Kennedy High School in Fremont, California. She regularly taught an English Literature course that included a unit on poetry. She had always wanted to teach an entire course on poetry—her passion—but she was never able to generate the necessary enrollments among students at Kennedy. VHS gave her the opportunity, and she used it to develop Poetry and Poetics for Publication. She said it took about the same time to develop and teach her VHS poetry course as it does to develop a more traditional course. However, she did say that additional time was needed to maintain the Web links for her course, since many Web sites were forced off the Web for copyright reasons.

Whereas Bergh felt that developing her VHS course took no more time than developing a regular course, Cynthia Costilla, the teacher at Allen High School who designed and taught Explorando varios aspectos de culturas hispanas reflected the sentiments of other teachers. She reported that designing her course took much more time than designing a face-to-face course. As she put it, "It's not like a regular course with a textbook where you just have to assign reading." She estimated that when she was posting new units to her course, it took her 2 to 2½ hours per day of effort. Pam Martin, Costilla's colleague at Allen and teacher of Earth 2525: A Time Traveler's Guide to Planet Earth, said, "I was working until 10:30 every night It takes more time to set it up than a regular course—it's like writing a book." Fortunately, this is a process that needs to happen only once for each course.

Teachers felt that they were prepared well for this new set of responsibilities by the Teachers Learning Conference. In our surveys, teachers reported that the TLC was effective in helping them design and teach their new courses. (Similarly, those teachers not developing their own courses reported that the NetCourse Instructional Methodologies [NIM] course effectively prepared them to teach a VHS course.)

However, even after their courses were up and running, VHS teachers often reported spending more time on their new VHS courses than their regular courses, in part out of interest and in part out of necessity. During their initial year teaching in VHS, two of our case study teachers reported spending 20 hours a week on their courses. David Jost, Westborough High School teacher of Music Appreciation and Composition, reported spending about 15 to 20 hours a week on his VHS course, about twice what he would spend on a regular course. After Cynthia Costilla developed her Spanish culture course, she spent about an hour a day at school and about 7 hours a week at home on the class. Pam Martin reported spending about 3½ hours a day on her class of 14 students. Terry Haugen, Miramonte High teacher of Russian, Soviet, and Post-Soviet Studies, said, "It's my life! From the time I'm up at 5:00 in the morning, I'm checking for messages and assignments, and as soon as I'm done teaching, I'm on the computer."

The effort required by the courses seems to become much more manageable in subsequent years, and VHS staff provide information to teachers in the TLC and NIM courses about how to manage their teaching time effectively. Nonetheless, almost all teachers in our surveys responded that their VHS courses took at least as much time to teach and manage as a typical regular course. Most teachers spent more time on their VHS course than a regular course but felt that the time and effort were justified. Sometimes the workload was exacerbated by the fact that many students were working on different parts of a course. The teacher of Creative Problem Solving said, "I've got kids handing in stuff from Chapter 3—we are on Chapter 14. . . . Right now I feel like I'm teaching 17 individual courses." Despite the challenge of the workload (and note that the VHS staff instructs teachers to keep students on a single schedule as much as possible, to avoid "teaching individual courses"), most VHS teachers expressed their excitement about VHS and their desire to continue teaching their virtual courses.

The time spent on VHS most often involves reading and responding to e-mail from students and other teachers, as well as preparing new course materials (such as multimedia documents), putting these materials online, and updating the course schedule. For example, after dinner each night, Anita Bergh signed on to her poetry course from home. She checked in with other VHS teachers, read the 25 or so student comments, and printed their assignments. Tracy Sheehan, the Bioethics teacher of our case study, estimated that she spent about 15 hours each week teaching her course during the first year, and less in subsequent years. Since all the course materials had been created during the summer, most of her time during the academic year was spent interacting with students and checking their work rather than creating or posting assignments. Most of this time was invested at home.

What Teachers Do in NetCourses

The flexibility of working with students from home was often cited by teachers (and students) as an advantage of VHS. A nearly unanimous response was that teachers in our surveys were satisfied with the amount of flexibility they had in teaching their VHS courses. The ability to work outside of the normal frenetic activity of the school day may be the reason that VHS teachers were able to give students the one-on-one attention that students often mentioned with praise. On the other hand, this ability (and perhaps necessity) to work at home may intrude on teachers' free time and add to the perception that participation in the VHS program is very demanding.

VHS teachers also spent their time interacting with other online teachers. Regular interaction among teachers is a characteristic feature of VHS, in contrast to bricks-and-mortar schools, where exchanging information with a colleague next door is often precluded by the immediate demands of a classroom full of students. From our surveys, we found that VHS teachers reported collaborating with other teachers and outside experts more often than they did in their regular courses. Much of this teacher–teacher interaction was the result of the TLC and the NIM, where teachers had access to VHS experts and to their colleagues from other VHS courses. Teachers in several of the VHS courses were able to take advantage of the Internet to collaborate with one or more colleagues located at other schools. For example, in the fall of 1997, both of the VHS teachers at Westborough High School had the benefit of working with a co-teacher at another location. Both of these teachers believed it was very helpful to have a colleague on whom they could draw as they learned to master a new medium and struggled with a variety of unfamiliar management issues. Tracy Sheehan said, "I think team teaching should be the norm." She and a co-teacher located hundreds of miles away became close friends and collaborators.

On the other hand, VHS teachers reported in our survey that they collaborated with parents less often in their VHS courses than in their regular courses—an unsurprising finding. Furthermore, VHS teachers rarely reported involving others outside of school—such as scientists, senior citizens, and businesspeople—in their virtual teaching. In our early surveys, a majority of superintendents, principals, and site coordinators had expressed a hope and expectation that these new participants would be included in virtual courses. This lack of connection to the outside world was not due to a lack of trying; several teachers expressed an interest in using the Internet to break out of the formal classroom boundaries. For example, Anita Bergh wanted to teach her poetry course in conjunction with a local community college. Terry Haugen had planned from the start to include Russian studies experts from the university and to collaborate with teachers and students from the Ukraine in her teaching of her Russian, Soviet, and Post-Soviet Studies course. However, Learning-Space, with its division of virtual space into password-protected classrooms, did not easily accommodate this innovative use of the Internet.

Despite the constraints of the software, we found in our surveys of teachers that the pedagogical strategies they used in their VHS NetCourses were quite similar to those they used in their regular courses. A large majority of VHS teachers reported using constructivist approaches in their teaching, in both their regular and VHS courses. Almost all teachers included at least some inquiry-based projects in their courses. They reported relating school learning in their courses to work experience or real-world situations (although not electronically connecting with people in work settings). Most said they engaged students in collaborative projects and writing reports that they shared electronically with the community or other audiences. All the VHS teachers reported that they used performance-based assessment activities or materials that measured knowledge, reasoning, collaboration, and self-reflection.

Students' Participation in NetCourses

Students also put a significant amount of effort into their VHS NetCourses, perhaps because, according to our student surveys, they are very satisfied with the VHS program and are able to take courses that are not available otherwise. In our surveys of teachers, they said that students spent about the same amount of time or more studying in their VHS courses as in their regular courses. Although teachers often felt that their VHS students did not turn in their work in a timely fashion (it is far easier to fall behind in a course when you don't see the teacher every day), teachers reported that VHS students had no more missing assignments than did regular students. Also from our surveys, we found that both teachers and site coordinators expressed satisfaction with the active engagement of students in their VHS courses. Sometimes, however, the level of engagement was a point of complaint among students. Several of the students in our case study focus groups expressed surprise at the higher-than-expected workload of their VHS courses. They also acknowledged the need for and difficulty of self-discipline; "Having discipline is tough," said one student. Nonetheless, most teachers indicated they were satisfied with the ability of students to work independently in their VHS courses.

Students in our case study focus groups indicated that they liked to be able to work when and where they wanted. Like teachers, they often did their work at home, where many had access to computers and the Internet. Some indicated that they liked the self-pacing of courses. In fact, one student at Westborough was a member of the American Olympic luge team and was able to stay active in school in part by taking two VHS courses while training with the team in Europe.

Creating a sense of connectedness among students in VHS courses was a challenge for teachers. Terry Haugen asked, "How do we personalize this? How do we make the kids more aware that there's a human being on the other side?" Teachers often met this challenge, according to students in our focus groups. The design of community-building activities, like those of Tracy Sheehan in Bioethics, is important. As a result, students in our focus groups usually felt that they received enough attention from their VHS teachers. Indeed, some felt that the attention was more personal than they would otherwise receive in their regular classes; in one remarkable instance, for example, a talented VHS teacher was able to understand from a student's postings in the CourseRoom that he was depressed and needed some counseling. On the other hand, the distance and relative anonymity of the virtual environment was sometimes helpful, as in Tracy Sheehan's Bioethics course, where she felt that students could better express their personal feelings and opinions about controversial topics because of the insulation VHS provided. But surprisingly often, students reported that they knew their virtual teacher and fellow students very well. As one student put it, "This is definitely *not* impersonal."

Students' sense of interpersonal connectedness often was due to the efforts of the site coordinator. There was an "in-school" component of the virtual experience, and this was the charge of the coordinators. In addition to their administrative work, coordinators spent much of their time working with individual students and their VHS teachers. Some coordinators would meet individually with each VHS student once a week to review progress, address concerns, and provide general support and encouragement. Cheryl Davis, the coordinator at Miramonte High School, asked students to keep a log of their work and experiences. She and other coordinators also acted as the intermediary with students' VHS teachers. They would follow up on inquiries from teachers about a lagging student, contact teachers who were unresponsive to students, or broker solutions when a student and teacher were unable to resolve a particular issue. This kind of personal attention evoked the comment from one student at Kennedy High School that Jerry Lapiroff, the site coordinator, was "the real teacher" in the VHS program.

Staying close to VHS students was a challenge for coordinators because students often worked on their courses at varying times of the day and some worked mainly at home. But in several schools, the coordinator recommended or required that VHS students do at least some of their work in the computer lab. These labs were sometimes open in the evenings or weekends for the convenience of students. According to our survey of coordinators, about half of them scheduled use of computer labs for the same time slot in the course schedule of all VHS students in their schools. In these cases, the site coordinator would circulate among the students while they were working on their course and offer them help and assistance. VHS students working in the same computer lab at the same time came to see each other as resources. They would help other students with their virtual courses, even though the students were enrolled in different courses. This help often focused on the challenges of using a new software environment. In addition, the computer labs sometimes had technical staff that could help students with their software problems.

Teachers in our surveys expressed satisfaction with the amount of interaction they had with students in VHS courses—about the same as that in their regular courses. However, teachers felt that the student-to-student interaction was less in their VHS courses than in their regular courses. Site coordinators concurred, responding that students interacted less often with both teachers and other students in their VHS courses than in their regular courses.

Generating a high level of student participation in the CourseRoom is a significant problem for VHS teachers. Many courses in our case studies had relatively little day-to-day online activity. This problem was documented by student and teacher comments, as well as our own observations of course activity on the Web. Students in four out of five focus groups in our first-year evaluation indicated that only a minority of students in their courses were online daily.

Cynthia Costilla estimated that only 5 of 11 students in her course were active on a regular basis. Terry Haugen estimated that only 4 of her 9 students that semester were online regularly. As one student at Allen High School put it, "I didn't think I would be taking a correspondence course, but that's what it is." Another student said, "It's not interactive at all." Nonetheless, students in our focus groups indicated a preference for more interaction rather than less, and they recognized its contribution to their learning.

Student Interaction and Collaboration in NetCourses

Often, the courses were not structured to encourage student-to-student interaction. Replicating the standard classroom, the dominant mode of communication was between the teacher and the students, individually or collectively. An analysis of the CourseRoom in a typical VHS course illustrates the nature of the interaction. There were 10 students enrolled in this social science course. There were 37 discussion topics posted in the CourseRoom; 19 of these were posted by the teacher and 18 by the students. These topics generated 138 postings during the semester. The students accounted for 94 of these postings, with a range of 2 to 20 per student and an average of 9.4 per student. However, just three students accounted for 47% of all the student postings. The pattern of these postings is even more telling. More than 75% of the students' comments were in direct response to an entry or posting made by the teacher. A large majority of the entries or postings made by students were addressed by the teacher. Only five student comments were in response to postings of other students. Most of the interaction was questions and answers between teachers and students. Although this pattern of interaction may have contributed to the students' sense that they received individual teacher attention, it generated very little in-depth discussion or sharing of ideas among students.

Student collaboration and small-group work was even more problematic online. Teachers reported that it was particularly challenging to structure their courses and activities to foster substantive student group work. Students at Miramonte High School agreed that even when teachers did a good job of structuring group work, collaboration was not always successful. The students cited one example of an assignment in which four students had to work together. The assignment did not work because some students were behind and some were having trouble with the technology. The group assignment in another course did not work because students did not sign on regularly. In yet another class, a group assignment did not work because everyone was at a different place in the course. (To be fair, high-quality group work is probably exceptional in most face-to-face courses, not only in netcourses.)

The low level of interaction described for many courses was not universal. For example, in Tracy Sheehan's Bioethics course, there were 45 discussion topics posted in the CourseRoom. These generated about 1,500 discussion postings. The 14 students in her course contributed from 7 to 180 discussion entries each. The 17 students in Anita Bergh's Poetry and Poetics course were also very active. At the time of a visit in October 1997, she had estimated that these were between 500 and 600 comments in the CourseRoom. She structured the course with frequent but brief assignments, and much student–student interaction related to these assignments. When appropriate, she would redirect students' private messages to the whole group so that they would stimulate discussion and everyone would benefit. She also kept close track of all the students' assignments and progress. Consequently, she felt that she knew each student individually, a perception confirmed by comments from her students at several other case study sites. Students at our other case study sites gave their perspective on the poetry course. A student at Westborough said the course was interesting, and she thought that Anita Bergh was highly responsive and "on top of things" in managing the course. Perhaps because of this level of involvement, none of her students dropped out of the course.

However, the level of student-to-student interaction varied from one subject to another or one teacher to another. For example, language arts and social science courses seemed to have a lot of online discussion. Computer Programming and Music Appreciation had relatively little. One student at Westborough—whose views were not necessarily shared by others—went so far as to say that mathematics was not a suitable subject for a virtual course because answering students' questions quickly is so important and because even posing a question may be difficult online. "I didn't understand that" makes a lot more sense if a student says it at a particular moment when a teacher is writing equations on a chalkboard or looking over a shoulder than it does as an online message to the teacher. Teachers also varied in the amount of interaction in their courses. One teacher who expressed frustration at not being able to structure group activities in VHS did not in general believe that group work and student-to-student interaction were important ways in which students learn. Indeed, she perceived some inherent unfairness in student group work (e.g., the free-rider problem), and she reported that she rarely provided students opportunities to collaborate in her face-to-face classes.

But teacher, course, and technique differences are not the only ones that explain the variation in the amount of interaction in a VHS course. Students also play a crucial role. There was much less interaction in the next offering of Poetry and Poetics. Anita Bergh expressed frustration about her limited ability to do something about it; "I can send the note, but they can choose to not respond, and I have no other recourse." The previous level of discussion made the course personal; with less discussion, she felt it was more like a correspondence course.

The asynchronous structure of the software environment contributed to the lack of interaction. Many students, even some who commented positively on teacher responsiveness, indicated a frustration with the slowness of interactions on the system. Answers to even the simplest questions might require a day or two for a response. Sometimes the need for this answer and the slowness of the response would impede students' progress in a course.

Anita Bergh was convinced that a chat capability would greatly enhance her VHS course, as were several other teachers. Although several of the various virtual-school software environments have chat functions, the version of Learn-ingSpace used by VHS does not. Students in our Kennedy High School focus group felt that the use of chat would allow them to get immediate feedback and would enable ideas to flow better. Students at Miramonte also felt a need for chat, although they acknowledged that it would be difficult to find a common time for this to happen across different time zones. But students in another one of our focus groups thought that even 1 hour of chat a week in a course would help. Of course, chat need not involve all students at one time, and finding common times for smaller groups (as small as two students, or the teacher and a single student) would be easier to arrange than for a whole class.

Comparison of VHS and Face-to-Face Courses

To extend our analysis of the VHS experience, we decided to compare VHS courses directly with comparable courses taught face to face by the same teacher. Although several of our survey questions asked instructors to make comparisons between their VHS and regular courses, we wanted to investigate more closely how courses and classroom experiences were similar and different.

The Four Courses Studied

Four VHS teachers participated in a study during the spring of 2000, each teaching their courses in both online and face-to-face modes. Two of the four courses were primarily academic; the other two were more career oriented. The courses examined for this study are displayed in Table 3.1.

Although this quasi-experimental study provides a unique opportunity to look at four VHS courses and their face-to-face counterparts side by side, the approach has an important qualification. The four courses we examined are not typical of VHS courses. According to administrators and teachers, the large majority of VHS courses could be offered only because they were online—that is, there were no face-to-face counterparts. Fewer than 10% of the 94 VHS courses being taught during 1999–2000 were also taught by the same teacher in a face-to-face version. It is quite possible that the online courses that were first offered as face-to-face courses may be more traditional than those courses designed specifically for the Internet, but the findings reported in the preceding

Table 3.1
NetCourses Included in the VHS/Face-to-Face Comparison Study

Title	Description of NetCourse	Comparison, VHS vs. Face-to-Face
Advanced Placement Statistics	AP Statistics runs a full year and prepares students for an examination that qualifies those who pass for college credit. The course introduces students to concepts and statistical tools for collecting and analyzing data and drawing conclusions.	The online and face-to-face versions of AP Statistics are essentially the same.
Modern Classics, Living Authors	This is a literary analysis course in which students interpret texts and write expository essays. The course texts, written by English and American authors, contain a number of related themes that the students explore throughout the course. Students do a good deal of reading, information processing, and essay writing offline or out of class.	The semester-long VHS course is derived from a year-long, face-to-face Advanced Placement English course, Modern Classics, with which it was compared.
Expanding Artistic Vision Through Photography	The course teaches the basic elements of photographic composition: vantage, frame, subject, breadth, and depth.	The one-semester VHS course is based on one segment of a two-year face-to-face photography career program. In the latter case, the photographic composition course follows one year of courses on film developing, printing, and lighting.
Pre-Engineering and Design	This is a "hands-on" laboratory course. The course introduces students to the basics of engineering design and problem solving. Students develop, design, and create prototype solutions to fictional design and engineering problems. Construction projects typically require inexpensive materials, such as cardboard, paper, tape, batteries, wire, and string.	The one-semester VHS course covers only a portion of the syllabus of the face-to-face course, which carries twice the credit. As a lab course, this NetCourse poses special challenges for instruction in an online environment.

section would suggest not. The hands-on nature of several of the courses in this study was also not typical of the majority of VHS NetCourses.

The study relied on interviews with teachers, surveys of students, and observations in both classroom- and Web-based versions of the courses. To assess the impact of the courses on student learning, SRI also examined student performance on two types of measures: teacher-generated "key assignments" and an assessment of Internet research skills. Outcome results related to these measures are reported in the next chapter. In this chapter, we focus on the virtual and face-to-face experiences.

Study Findings

The first thing that we found was a number of differences in the nature of the VHS courses themselves, as compared with their face-to-face counterparts. Adjustments were necessary to put the courses online. For example, content in three of the VHS courses (Modern Classics, Photographic Vision, and Pre-Engineering) was a subset of more complete courses taught face to face. Also, assignments were sometimes modified in VHS courses, and VHS students often had less time for and/or spent less time on assignments than students in the face-to-face courses. Nonetheless, the content in VHS courses was a substantial subset of the content in regular courses; and for the common segments, the VHS courses had the same or similar goals, content, structure, and assignments as their corresponding face-to-face courses.

Students in both groups expressed interest in and enjoyment of their courses. VHS students were likely to agree that their VHS courses were of high quality and required hard work, but face-to-face students were more likely to agree strongly with these statements about their courses.

The student dropout rate was low for both sets of courses but slightly lower for the face-to-face courses than for the VHS courses. VHS students were online regularly, and the technology provided access to some unique online materials in two VHS courses (AP Statistics and Modern Classics). Also, VHS students were more likely than face-to-face students to use the World Wide Web. But there were no significant differences between the groups in their other computer, e-mail, or general Internet use. There also were no reported differences between the two groups in the use of computers to do research projects or write reports as part of their coursework.

There were no significant differences between the two groups of students in the frequency of communication with teachers that they reported. However, face-to-face students were likely to agree strongly that discussion was a regular part of their courses, that they frequently communicated with other students, and that communication with other students was an important part of their learning. VHS students were likely to disagree with all of these statements. Also, teachers reported and we observed that, compared with face-to-face courses, the interaction among students and between students and their teachers in VHS courses was less in quantity and lower in quality.

The nature and quality of interaction were particularly problematic in the two courses for which student products required visual inspection by the teachers. This problem seemed to be due, in large part, to limitations in the capabilities of the technology relative to the needs of these courses. In the Photographic Vision course, students were required to use a camera. The VHS students used a digital camera and posted their photographs online, whereas the face-to-face students used professional camera and darkroom equipment. Both groups presented their work to their peers. But in the face-to-face version of the course, students discussed each other's photos in depth and frequently reshot their photographs in response to other students' critiques. By contrast, in the VHS version of the course, it was far more difficult for the same teacher to foster a culture of constructive critique. As the teacher put it, "I wanted them to talk less about it being a 'great picture,' more about what they are trying to accomplish with the photo." Too often, the comments were "Nice picture, dude" rather than "You really use the [photographic concept of the] frame well." The LearningSpace technology itself was part of the problem because the linear, asynchronous discussion structure was not sufficiently interactive to enable students to respond to one another quickly. Also, students were not able to make or see comments at the same time that they viewed photographs, nor could they communicate their critiques by gesturing or pointing to elements of a photograph.

Similarly, in the Pre-Engineering course, the quality of interaction differed dramatically between the VHS and face-to-face classes. In both, the teacher presented a problem (e.g., to design or build something), the students worked on it, and then there was a final presentation and critique. However, in the face-to-face class, students could observe the difficulties with prototypes created by their peers and learn from the teacher's critiques. Such dynamic demonstration and troubleshooting were not available in the VHS system. This is similar to an observation made by the VHS teacher from New Hanover High School. He expressed frustration with his inability to "just show them" when students encountered a problem in his VHS Computer Technology course. Perhaps as a result of this difficulty, VHS students posed many fewer questions to the teacher in the Pre-Engineering course than their face-to-face counterparts did.

Courses that require students to engage in hands-on work, particularly with media other than text, pose special challenges in an online environment. This is not to say that such courses cannot be successful, because they can, but they require special care and careful planning on the part of the teacher. For example, for several years we observed a VHS course called Music Appreciation and Composition, taught by David Jost at Westborough High School in Massachusetts. Each student in the course was issued a keyboard to connect with a computer, and students uploaded and downloaded music files in the "MIDI" format. The idea of making music composition the subject of a virtual high school course was, to us at least, rather surprising. However, although the teacher had to work hard—even in the second year, he spent about twice as much time each week on the virtual course as on any of his regular courses—the course was successful for many students who took it. In addition, David Jost's success was featured in an article in *U.S. News & World Report.*

Conclusions

It is clear from our surveys, case studies, and now this VHS/face-to-face study that online courses are similar in many ways to courses taught in bricks-and-mortar classrooms. Teachers prepare materials, provide guidance, and give and grade assignments. Students study materials, complete assignments, and engage in discussions. However, it is also clear that the limitations of today's commonly available online technologies create real problems for online teachers and students, particularly in some courses and particularly with respect to the ways in which participants interact with one another. What does it take for teachers to address these challenges and produce a high-quality online course experience?

What Makes a Good Virtual Course?

By 1999, the number of courses in the VHS catalog had begun to grow appreciably, and the VHS staff, teachers, and coordinators had begun to amass a significant body of experience with VHS courses. The VHS staff wanted to capture that experience and formulate it into a set of findings that would define the character of a high-quality online course.

The Expert Panel

To this end, in 1999, SRI formed and brought together a panel of six subject-matter area experts to help define a high-quality netcourse and to conduct course reviews. The panel was selected to include members with expertise in the core high school subject disciplines (specifically science/mathematics, English/language arts, and the social sciences) and also in standards development. As a group, the panel had many decades of secondary-level teaching experience (including several individuals with long tenure as department chairs), as well as impressive state and national experience in the development and application of standards for curriculum, instruction, and assessment.

The panel did its work over a period of 5 months. After first becoming familiar with the Virtual High School, the panel was able to reach consensus on a set of standards against which courses could be reviewed to determine their quality. These standards (see Table 3.2) draw on national standards in the disciplines (e.g., the National Council of Teachers of Mathematics *Principles and Standards for School Mathematics*) but are unusual in that they are designed to be cross-cutting, across both discipline areas and types of courses (such as elective versus required core courses). For example, the panel members agreed that all VHS courses should teach critical-thinking skills—regardless of whether the topic is science or language arts, or whether the course is a one-semester elective or a full-year advanced placement course.

In applying these standards, 18 VHS courses were initially selected for the panel to review. The sample included only courses that were developed and offered during VHS's first year of implementation (1997–1998) *and* that were also taught in later years. This continuity meant that each course had the opportunity to be further developed and refined after its initial implementation. Further, the selection of courses focused only on those courses that fell into the core discipline areas identified above. From among 18 courses that met these criteria, 12 were selected at random.

Panel Reviews

The panel used an exacting process to review these dozen courses. The standards document developed by the panel required each reviewer to rate a course against 19 individual standards, organized into four areas: Curriculum/Content, Pedagogy, Course Design, and Assessment of Students' Work. Reviewers rated each individual standard on a scale of 1 (low) to 4 (high). The course review rubric also provided space for comments (which turned out to be extensive), as well as for an overall course rating. The overall rating was a summary of course quality: A score of 3 indicates the course is of "high quality"; a score of 2 indicates the course is "satisfactory, but certain questions or issues need to be addressed"; and a score of 1 indicates the course quality is "of serious concern." Each course was reviewed and rated by two panel members. Table 3.3 summarizes their overall course ratings.

All but 1 of the 12 courses were rated as satisfactory or better. Six of the 12 were rated as "high quality," and another 4 were rated as "satisfactory." Only 1 of the 12 courses was rated "of serious concern" by reviewers. In addition, there was one instance in which reviewers could not agree on the overall rating; one reviewer rated the course "satisfactory" while the other rated it "high quality" (as indicated by ½ in the table). Table 3.4 displays the distribution of raters' scores across the categories of standards.

The panel found that there were high-quality VHS courses in every disciplinary area examined (mathematics/science, English/language arts, and social sciences). Themes in the types of elements present in these high-quality courses

Table 3.2

Standards for NetCourses, Developed by the SRI Expert Panel

STANDARD	EXAMPLE
Curriculum/Content	
1. The course facilitates learning about important information, skills, and major ideas from multiple viewpoints.	Major facts and ideas are taught.
2. The course models and emphasizes skills, tools, abilities, values, and habits of mind in the field being studied.	E.g., in a history course students might learn to use primary sources and timelines, and to judge events in historical context.
3. The course provides a considered treatment of breadth and depth.	Students will learn both a general understanding of the discipline and greater depth of comprehension about selected ideas and issues in the subject.
4. The course is designed so that students demonstrate comprehension of important ideas.	Describing, summarizing, interpreting, discussing, or extending facts and ideas presented in the course.
5. The course is designed to infuse critical thinking and problem solving.	Students apply new knowledge, analyze new situations, relate knowledge from several areas, create new ideas from old ones, etc.
6. The materials, activities, and assignments are well matched to the capabilities of students in the grade level(s); prerequisites are specified.	The difficulty level indicated in the course catalog matches the actual nature of the required work.
7. The course description is accurate and understandable to prospective students and other interested parties.	The course catalog description is accurate and complete.
8. Any controversial issues or materials are treated in a responsible manner.	Teachers don't confuse fact, theory, and opinion. Reasonable alternative viewpoints are not discouraged.

Table 3.2 (continued)

STANDARD	EXAMPLE
Pedagogy	
9. The course encourages an active approach to learning the subject, including interaction with the teacher and with other students.	Students are asked to do more than complete assignments and submit them to the teacher.
10. The course helps students make effective use of the medium.	The teacher is interacting online frequently; students are expected to be "present" frequently.
11. The course integrates multiple methods of instruction.	Examples include assigned reading, discussions, simulation, laboratories, assigned writing, critiques, peer review, presentations.
12. The course orchestrates discourse and collaboration among students within an environment in which multiple viewpoints/values are acknowledged and critically analyzed.	Students are encouraged to be active course participants; some assignments encourage collaboration; the teacher uses his or her "voice" appropriately; students feel safe expressing their opinions.
Course Design	
13. The course is structured in such a way that organization of course and use of medium are adequately explained and accommodating to needs of students.	Instructions take into account varied levels of familiarity with the technology.
14. All required course materials are made available to students.	Materials are sent to students or are made available to them on the Web.
15. The course schedule includes a listing of high-quality assignments that relate well to course objectives and activities.	Assignments are clearly listed with expected due dates.
16. The structure of the course encourages regular feedback.	Students receive regular feedback on their work.
17. The teacher clearly identifies performance objectives for students that will be used to assess their work in the course.	The teacher makes clear what constitutes success and how grades will be assigned.

Table 3.2 (continued)

STANDARD	EXAMPLE
Assessment of Students' Work	
18. Assessments are based on multiple indicators, which reflect multiple dimensions of students' learning.	Grades are based on more than a handful of assignments.
19. The course appropriately guides students toward reflection on their own learning.	Students are asked to evaluate their work.

* Each reviewer rated each standard according to the following scale:
Not Present or Evident in the NetCourse = 1, Somewhat Evident = 2, Clearly
Evident = 3, Exemplary = 4, Not Applicable to this NetCourse = 0

emerged from the reviews. High-quality courses, in the expert panel's opinion, encompass some combination of the following characteristics:

- *Important course content.* All courses should include a focus on critical thinking and problem solving, as well as an emphasis on important information, skills, and major ideas. An appropriate balance needs to be maintained between depth and breadth.
- *Effective and appropriate use of the medium.* Presentation of materials is clear, students are provided access to a variety of resources and perspectives with the appropriate tools to help examine them, and the use of the medium is sufficiently flexible that students can accomplish diverse tasks both online and offline.

Table 3.3
Overall Course Ratings

Overall Rating	Number of Courses (Number of Individual Reviews)
High quality	6 ½ (13)
Satisfactory quality	4 ½ (9)
Of serious concern	1 (2)
Total reviews	**12 (24)**

Table 3.4
Percentage Distribution of Standard Ratings

	0	1	2	3	4	Total Number of Ratings
Curriculum/ Content	2%	1%	11%	38%	**48%**	192
Pedagogy	0%	2%	26%	**39%**	33%	96
Course design	0%	4%	23%	**40%**	33%	120
Assessment	0%	6%	27%	**44%**	23%	48
Frequency totals	1%	2%	19%	**39%**	**39%**	456

Individual standard ratings: 0 is N/A; 1 is "Not Evident"; 2 is "Somewhat Evident"; 3 is "Clearly Evident"; 4 is "Exemplary."
Note: Modal responses, by row, are shown in bold.

- *Effective use of teacher's voice within the medium.* E.g., the teacher creates a structure to engage students in real substance and deep intellectual dialogue, and also creates an environment that facilitates sustained interaction and collaboration (e.g., student-to-student as well as student-to-teacher interaction).
- *Diverse and multiple methods of instruction.* E.g., a range of activities and assignments are presented, from problem solving to simulation to reader response, in order to consistently engage students throughout the course.
- *Quick, timely, regular feedback.* E.g., the teacher provides a continuous assessment of student work, including feedback on reasons why things are marked wrong and suggestions for improvement.
- *Clear objectives and performance expectations.* E.g., benchmarks and models of performance are provided and made clear up front, and teachers have mechanisms in place for keeping students on track.

Reviewing the Bioethics Symposium

Let us return to the course that we examined at the beginning of the chapter to see how the panel members applied these criteria to characterize the Bioethics course. Recall that both reviewers rated this course as "high" in overall quality. What made Bioethics an outstanding course? The panel members agreed that the course accomplished the goal of developing critical thinking and student inquiry. Regarding the effective and appropriate use of the medium, one reviewer said, "Though much of the course material was made available to students through course lessons and the MediaCenter, students were also required to make frequent use of Web sites and other media materials from their own environment." Regarding effective use of the teacher's voice in structuring the course, he went on to say, "The instructor made very effective use of student collaboration. . . . They worked together effectively in groups and teams." The other reviewer commented, "I found many tasks which directly tell students to view the work of others." Both reviewers found that Bioethics effectively used a variety of methods. As one review put it:

> The number and diversity of activities in the course designed to engage students actively in the substance of bioethics was very impressive: case studies, role playing, Web searches, creating a logo and cartoon, surveys, persuasive essay writing, simulations of a national hearing, bioethics symposium presentations, creation of Web pages. The course design not only kept the course interesting and moving, but it also seemed to engage students in a way that kept them on schedule rather than falling behind.

The other reviewer commented:

> Both the use of student journals (required weekly entry) and personal design of many activities (such as surveys to parents, friends, and teachers) encouraged students to reflect about their findings and to become personally involved with the ideas in the course. Writing a persuasive essay and applying the ethical systems standards to a movie, fairy tale, or story from their own experience were other indications of how this vehicle was used to engage learners in thinking about their learning.

The feedback in the course was also timely. "The instructor was prompt in giving feedback to students and commenting on their work," said one reviewer. Finally, regarding clear objectives and performance expectations, one reviewer commented, "The weekly What's My Grade feature was a means to provide some accountability to students about expectations and due dates." The other said, "I liked the inclusion of the rubrics for the weeks 7 and 11. This helps students get a sense of what is expected."

Clearly, Tracy Sheehan had crafted her Bioethics course to stimulate student thinking and learning effectively. Although not every one of the dozen courses that the panel examined was rated as high as Bioethics, overall, members of the panel were impressed by what they found. After spending many person-weeks examining the VHS courses in depth, the panel summed up its impressions of VHS by saying:

> The panel applauds the efforts of teachers and students who are pioneers in developing courses on the Internet that are challenging, interesting, and relevant. We see the project as beneficial in improving education by offering opportunities for a varied curriculum in schools with limited ability to do so. We hope that VHS will continue to grow and reach an even more diverse audience of schools and students. (Yamashiro & Zucker, 1999, p. ix)

Experiences in Other Online Programs

How is the VHS experience similar to experiences in other online schools? This is difficult to say, since few online schools let outside researchers through their virtual doors. Florida Virtual School is the only other online school that has opened its doors to outside evaluators (Bigbie & McCarroll, 2000). The results from their study suggest that the VHS experience may be typical of that in the Florida Virtual School. Students in both programs have positive opinions about their experience and feel that they are able to take courses that they would not be able to take otherwise. Both groups feel they do as much work in their virtual courses as in their regular courses. Both enjoy the flexibility of time and place that an online course provides. Both appreciate the interaction they have with their teachers. And—significantly—both groups feel that interaction with other students leaves something to be desired.

For other virtual programs, there are only brief descriptions on corporate Web sites to draw on. On the basis of these resources, it seems that the Apex experience may be similar to the VHS experience. As mentioned in this chapter, the Apex software environment has many of the same features as the VHS environment. It seems that students have access to hands-on activities and multimedia presentations, such as tutorials, explorations, and slide shows. They turn in their assignments online or by fax, and they are graded by the course instructor. Instructors take advantage of chat rooms, bulletin boards, and e-mail to create discussion in the class.

However, the IEI experience seems very different. It appears that much of the learning in the IEI courses occurs through online, self-instructional materials. This is certainly the case with the Parent-Directed option. Here students study on their own, with the supervision of a parent or local mentor provided by the parent. Students get feedback on their computer-graded tests. Even in the Instructor-Assisted option, the classroom interaction in IEI seems limited. With this option, students meet with their instructor and other students for 1 hour a week. Students have access to the instructor at other times, via e-mail, and to other students in the IEI learning center. This type of experience seems very different from the one in Tracy Sheehan's VHS course, where she designed Bioethics, structures the students' day-to-day activities, and takes personal responsibility for the quality of the course experience. "Who *should* take the responsibility?" she asked.

Conclusions

What is our assessment of the VHS experience? The most striking observation is that the online experience has many similarities to the experience in bricks-and-mortar schools. Teachers spend a lot of time preparing materials, interacting with students, and grading assignments. They use the same kinds of pedagogical techniques as they do in their regular courses. They engage students in inquiry-based projects, relate school learning to the real world, and have students write essays. Students spend as much time studying for their VHS courses as they do for their regular courses. They read materials, prepare assignments, and engage in discussions. Students feel connected to their teachers and to other students.

However, unlike the regular school experience, teachers are more likely to interact and collaborate with other teachers in VHS. They have and enjoy the flexibility of being able to work when and where they want. And they are able to teach courses that they would not be able to teach in their schools otherwise. Similarly, students enjoy the flexibility of VHS and the ability to take courses that are not otherwise available.

What is the role of technology in the virtual-school experience? Although technology plays the essential role of allowing courses to be offered and taken that would not be available otherwise, teachers and students are often confronted by its limitations. Because of the technology, as currently configured, teachers are less likely to collaborate with parents and rarely involve others in their teaching. They are frustrated that they cannot show things to students and that it is difficult to structure student discussion and collaboration. Students want more interaction, but their group work is often ineffective, and their electronic discussions often lack substance and are limited to exchanges with the teacher. These limitations sometimes make it difficult or impossible to teach certain kinds of courses effectively.

When the VHS courses succeed—as they often do—the success is due more than anything else to the effort and artful tinkering of capable and effective teachers and site coordinators, who have been well prepared in VHS's online professional development courses. Teachers, coordinators, and students have to overcome considerable technological, logistical, and motivational challenges. Teachers design important content and use the medium to present it effectively. They use a variety of instructional methods and structure situations to engage students in deep intellectual dialogue. They present clear objectives and provide timely feedback. Site coordinators meet with students individually and in groups. They monitor their progress and encourage their efforts. Students work on assignments, delve into discussions, and exercise self-discipline. When all these challenges are met, teachers, coordinators, and students partake in a thought-provoking, highly interpersonal, enriching, and rewarding virtual experience.

Chapter 4

OUTCOMES OF A VIRTUAL SCHOOL

For those people who are still dubious about the appeal or value of learning online, the high levels of satisfaction expressed by VHS participants must come as a surprise. For example, fewer than one in five students were *not* satisfied with their VHS experience. About 80% of students reported that they would like to take another online course through VHS, and an even higher percentage were ready to recommend VHS to other students. The satisfaction that students, teachers, school principals, and others express about VHS is an important outcome of their experiences, because otherwise they would not continue to participate in the school. This chapter begins with a look at data about VHS participants' satisfaction with the online school.

However, judging the value of a virtual school involves more than just answering the question of whether or not the students and others like their experiences. Not only skeptics but anyone interested in knowing more about online schools will want to have answers to such questions as: How hard did students work, and how much did they learn? Do experienced educators working with the students, such as teachers and VHS coordinators, believe that virtual courses have the same value to students as face-to-face courses? Are there test scores to compare what students learn online versus face to face? These and related questions about the value of online learning for students are addressed in the second section. Next, the chapter explores the outcomes of the VHS experience for participating teachers and administrators, many of whom believe that they, too, have benefited from VHS. Finally, the chapter examines what is known about outcomes in other virtual schools and offers conclusions about the entire set of outcomes.

Participants' Satisfaction with VHS

According to survey and interview data, satisfaction with VHS increased over time, as start-up problems were overcome, norms and routines were established, and the participants became more comfortable with what was a new medium for almost everyone. Some of these increases in satisfaction occurred as early as the second year of operation. Those who are interested in starting to teach or provide online courses for the first time should understand that the first year is likely to be distinctly different from subsequent years, presenting more problems and requiring more hard work.

In fact, the most notable evaluation findings for the second year of opera tion were those related to the level of satisfaction with VHS expressed by participants. All participant groups expressed greater satisfaction with the VHS project during the second year of operation than during the first year. Among superintendents, principals, teachers, and site coordinators, the percentages of respondents who were either somewhat satisfied or very satisfied with the VHS project were very similar (92%, 96%, 97%, and 100%, respectively). Compared with the first year, many more participants expressed being "very satisfied" with VHS. The increase in teacher satisfaction with VHS overall was statistically significant ($t = 3.11$, $p < .0029$). Because VHS teachers must work hard to master a new medium and because they are the ones most responsible for creating and delivering high-quality courses, their satisfaction with the VHS experience is important. And, as noted at the beginning of this chapter, students also express a high degree of satisfaction with their VHS experiences.

Over time, teachers reported that their NetCourses became better. For example, teachers were asked to rate their satisfaction with their regular classroom courses on the same 4-point scale as their VHS NetCourses (1 meaning very satisfied and 4 meaning not at all satisfied). In contrast to findings in VHS's first year (1997–1998), when teachers' ratings of satisfaction were significantly higher for their regular classroom courses than for their VHS courses, by the next school year their ratings of satisfaction with the quality of the two types of courses were almost the same (mean scale rating: VHS 1.4; regular 1.3). In some respects, teachers are even more satisfied with their VHS courses than with their regular courses. For example, in the 2000–2001 school year, 6% of the VHS teachers reported that they were not very satisfied with the level of challenge and rigor of the face-to-face courses they were teaching, compared with only 3% who felt the same way about their online course.

Nonetheless, as was pointed out in Chapters 2 and 3, teachers continue to view certain specific aspects of NetCourses, such as promoting student-to-student interaction, as less satisfying—meaning less effective—than comparable activities in face-to-face courses. Similarly, just as the teachers rated the Teachers Learning Conference (TLC) very highly overall (with only 3% of the respondents to the 2000–2001 survey reporting that it was not very or not at all effective in preparing them to teach online), fully one-fourth found that the TLC did not prepare them very effectively to include successful group activities in their VHS courses. This response almost certainly is more of a commentary on the difficulty of conducting group activities in LearningSpace than it is about deficits in the TLC per se. For example, one teacher said that students "do not like group work due to the fact that some students won't do their part, or won't even log on until the project is almost due." Managing group work effectively is hard for many teachers even in face-to-face classes, and it is harder online.

Within the context of overall satisfaction with VHS, another area of concern for teachers and coordinators is with administrative procedures and the software used for enrolling and for dropping students from VHS courses. For example, nearly 40% of the teachers in school year 2000–2001 were not very or at all satisfied with the software and procedures for enrolling students. One teacher wrote: "Registration needs to be improved. It is very hard to teach a 15-week course when students come into class [the course] late because they were taken off wait lists. Sometimes students are not notified that they are off the wait list." Teachers' lack of satisfaction with procedures for dropping students is also discussed in the section of this chapter that examines students' persistence and grades in online courses.

Taken together, the data show that although there are some specific areas of weakness, participants are generally very satisfied with VHS. The fact that there are a great many repeaters—students taking multiple courses, teachers continuing to be involved for years, and so on—and that VHS continues to grow are perhaps the most convincing pieces of evidence that the virtual school provides a satisfying experience for the large majority of participants.

Outcomes of Students' Participation in VHS Courses

Students' satisfaction is a tribute to the hard work and expertise of the VHS teachers and the careful attention paid to a myriad of details related to operating a virtual school. Nonetheless, learning—not satisfaction—must be the bottom line for schools. Learning takes effort, and it is therefore important to find that more than three-fourths of the VHS students reported that they worked as hard or harder in the VHS courses as in face-to-face courses.

Reports About Students' Learning

What is more, students believe that they learned a great deal by taking VHS courses. Nearly 90% of students said that their participation was a valuable learning experience and that they learned a substantial amount of new subject matter. The VHS teachers agreed, with only a few teachers reporting that they were not very satisfied with their students' engagement in the online courses or with the amount that the students learned. Similarly, the VHS coordinators— who have a somewhat different perspective than VHS teachers do because they often become familiar with a dozen or more of the online courses—agreed that VHS students learned about the same amount as, or even more than, in their regular, face-to-face courses. Almost a third of the coordinators indicated that students learned *more* in VHS courses than in those same students' regular courses, while about half observed little difference between the two types of offerings. Only 17% of the site coordinators reported that students learned less in VHS courses than they did in face-to-face courses.

The teachers reported that VHS students' ability to grasp and learn the subject material was comparable to what students were able to do in face-to-face courses. Similarly, nearly 90% of the teachers reported that they were satisfied or very satisfied with the extent to which VHS students were actively engaged with the content of the courses, corresponding closely to the teachers' opinions about the students in these teachers' face-to-face courses.

Significantly, the degree of teachers' satisfaction with students' online learning has increased over the years that VHS has been offering NetCourses. A variety of explanatory factors are probably at work, ranging from more effective selection of student participants to an increased understanding of how online courses need to be structured and taught if high school students are to be successful in them.

It is important to keep in mind that students are learning material in VHS courses that otherwise would not be available to them. For example, more than 90% of the coordinators reported that most VHS students took courses that they would not have been able to take otherwise. Gaining access to new courses is a key motivation for all the VHS participants, and many participants might be satisfied even if they learned somewhat less than in face-to-face courses. However, the more common view of people considering whether or not to participate in virtual schools is likely to be that students should learn as much in online courses as they do in their regular courses.

Student Test Data

In spite of the unanimity of opinion about the value to students of enrolling in VHS courses, it would be useful to have hard data about students' achievement in these online courses, such as test scores. Such data, if it were positive, would add weight to the argument that online learning can be effective for high school students. However, the Virtual High School faces a dilemma in trying to collect such data, because the great majority of the courses are electives that are not part of the core curriculum. Given that there are no national standardized tests for high school classes in poetry, or Russian studies, or bioethics, neither VHS staff nor the evaluators have been able to administer or report students' scores on such tests.

One important exception is that VHS has offered a few advanced placement (AP) courses. It is clear from the experience of VHS that an online advanced placement course can successfully prepare students to take and pass the AP exam. For example, in both the face-to-face and the VHS versions of the

AP Statistics course offered by the same teacher during the 1999–2000 school year, 40% of the students who attempted the AP exam received passing scores (3 or higher on a 5-point scale). In fact, the highest AP scores among these two groups were received by students in the VHS version of the course.

As noted in earlier chapters, a number of other virtual high schools also offer AP courses and have found that students can pass AP examinations after completing these online courses. For example, evaluators for the Florida Virtual School report that in the 1999–2000 school year, "of the 45 FVS students that took the [AP] exam and reported their score to the school, 69% earned a score of three or more" (Bigbie & McCarroll, 2000, p. 181). The AP data provide convincing evidence that online courses can prepare students to do well on the standardized AP tests.

In the future, more data will become available about the percentages of students in online and face-to-face courses who attempt the AP test (which usually is not required of students taking AP courses), how they do, and the comparability of the students who enroll in regular versus online AP courses. For the present, it is impossible to say that online AP courses are just as good for *all* students as face-to-face courses. As long as the number of high school students in the online AP courses is measured in such small numbers, generalizing to a population of hundreds of thousands or millions of students involves many uncertainties.

In addition to reviewing data about satisfaction, participants' perceptions of the value of online courses, and AP test score data, the evaluation team also studied the question of how much students learn online in several other ways. Chapter 3 included information about a study comparing four VHS courses with comparable courses taught face to face by the same teachers. The next two sections report on student outcome data gathered through this study.

Comparing Outcomes in VHS and Face-to-Face Courses

Chapter 3 included information about four VHS courses that were also taught face to face by the same teachers: AP Statistics, Modern Classics, Photographic Vision, and Pre-Engineering. To assess the impact of these courses on student learning, SRI examined student performance on two types of measures: teacher-generated "key assignments" and an assessment of Internet research skills. The key assignment was an important test, paper, or project selected by the teachers from those that were assigned to students in both versions of the courses. These assignments were unique to each course. Our analyses used both the teachers' scores or grades on these assignments and those from qualified external graders hired by SRI. The external graders used the teachers' rubrics to independently rescore the assignments, without knowing whether the students were from the face-to-face or VHS versions of the courses. Only three courses were used in these analyses because it was not possible for both the teacher and the independent graders to score the hands-on assignments of the VHS students in the Pre-Engineering course.

Especially in light of the small number of courses examined, there are many potential differences between the two versions of the courses that might influence student outcomes, such as differences in students' characteristics or their dropout rates. Indeed, important differences did exist between the online and face-to-face students:

- There were significant differences in student characteristics between the two versions of the career-oriented courses (Photographic Vision and Pre-Engineering), according to teachers. VHS students were reported to be better prepared academically than students in the corresponding face-to-face courses. On the other hand, the students in the face-to-face photography course were more focused on a career in that field, whereas VHS students approached the topic more as a hobby.
- Comparing the VHS and face-to-face groups, VHS students were more likely to be 11th-graders, and face-to-face students were more likely to be 12th-graders.
- VHS students were more likely to be enrolled in six or more courses than were face-to-face students. Consequently, their VHS courses were often taken on top of a full course schedule.

Such factors confound a study and make it difficult to attribute causality to one particular approach or the other. Nonetheless, the comparisons resulted in some interesting and valuable findings.

Across the three pairs of courses that were included in the key assignment analysis, there were no significant differences in teacher scores (grades) between the face-to-face students and the VHS students. Also, there were no significant differences in the external graders' scores between the face-to-face and VHS students in two of the three courses. However, the face-to-face students in the Photographic Vision course (students who were preprofessional) were scored significantly higher by the independent grader than VHS students taking the same course. The evidence is thus mixed, but it does tend to reinforce the view that students can learn just as much online as face to face. At the same time, as noted in Chapter 3, some courses seem less well suited to presentation online than others.

Learning Information Management and Technology Skills

An Internet research assessment was designed by SRI to measure the impact of regular computer use on students' skills with technology use, reasoning with information, and communication. These are skills identified by the U.S. Department of Labor as being important to the information society of the future by the Secretary's Commission on Necessary Skills (2000) and by other groups. Students in the same four VHS and face-to-face courses identified above were asked to volunteer for this assessment; those who did were compensated. The Internet assessment was delivered online. These students also filled out an online questionnaire.

Both face-to-face and VHS students in all four courses took the same Internet performance assessment. The evaluation team chose a task for the design of the Internet assessment instrument that has at its core the "active processing of information" (Means & Olson, 1995), because educators and psychologists widely agree that expertise in a field as well as advanced skills of comprehension, composition, reasoning, and experimentation are developed by the kind of active processing that the assessment was designed to assess (Bransford, Brown, & Cocking, 1999; Collins, Brown, & Newman, 1989; Resnick, 1987). The assessment that was designed was called "Choose-a-City." The premise was that a foreign exchange student wanted the student subjects to recommend which of two cities would be better to live in for a summer, with the possibility of permanently moving there later. The exchange student was interested in the cities' recreational opportunities, public transportation systems, and economies. To gather information on which to base their recommendations, the student subjects were given links to the two cities' official home pages to begin their search, but they could go anywhere they wanted on the Web from there. For each of the two cities, on each topic of interest, students had to select from a choice of four ratings and then cite two pieces of evidence to support their rating and provide the URLs to the Web pages that contained the evidence. They then answered three questions directed at seeing how well, in the course of their Web research, they could find a piece of questionable information, explain why it was questionable, generate a line of inquiry for checking the information's credibility, and generate a query that would launch them on an effective search. Finally, the students were asked to compose a letter to the foreign exchange student recommending a city and explaining why.

A complex scoring rubric was applied to the students' responses to the Choose-a-City assignment. Ten different components of the assessment task were identified, and a passing criterion was identified for each of them. For example, student subjects each recommended one of the cities to the fictional foreign exchange student; to pass on the "rating evidence" component, a subject's response had to be consistent with the evidence that he or she cited. Overall, more than 80% of the subjects did pass on this portion of the assessment task.

Findings and Conclusions. The students' performances were independently scored by two raters, and the mean score between the two was used for analysis. The scores were analyzed on a pass/no-pass basis. Table 4.1 displays

Table 4.1

Number and Percent "Pass" on Internet Research Assessment for VHS and Face-to-Face Courses

	Summary				
		VHS		Face to Face	
Skill Area	**Component**	**N Pass**	**% Pass**	**N Pass**	**% Pass**
Technology Use	Citing URL	28 (29)	97	22 (27)	81
	Formulating search query	24 (28)	86	16 (24)	67
	Total passes	*52 (57)*	*91*	*38 (51)*	*75*
Reasoning with Information	Rating evidence	26 (29)	90	25 (32)	78
	Finding questionable information	17 (26)	65	16 (24)	67
	Generating research question	22 (28)	79	19 (24)	79
	Total passes	*65 (83)*	*78*	*60 (80)*	*75*
Communication	Organization	26 (29)	90	20 (27)	74
	Support	27 (29)	93	19 (27)	70
	Drawing conclusions	25 (29)	86	18 (27)	67
	Mechanics	24 (29)	83	21 (27)	78
	Used own words	29 (29)	100	27 (27)	100
	Total passes	*131 (145)*	*90*	*105 (135)*	*78*

Note: Numbers of students' scores from the assessment components are shown in parentheses.

the scores. Unsurprisingly, the most pronounced difference between the groups was on the skill area of technology use. In every course, more VHS students than face-to-face students passed this portion of the assessment. Another major difference occurred in the Photographic Vision and Pre-Engineering courses. Many more VHS students than face-to-face students passed all of the skill areas of the Internet assessment. Also, on the skill area of reasoning with information, the VHS students in the AP Statistics course performed better than did the face-to-face students. In only one course, on only one skill area, did face-to-face students outperform VHS students: in the Modern Classics course, more face-to-face students than VHS students passed the skill area of reasoning with information. On the basis of all the data, it is reasonable to say that the VHS students in these courses acquired more of the skills needed for the information society than the face-to-face students did.

Across all the VHS courses, the students' opinions about learning to use computer technology are consistent with these findings from the four courses that were taught both online and face to face. Three-fourths of all VHS students reported that their skills using computer technology improved a lot as a result of participating in VHS. The VHS coordinators provide an independent verification of this finding, with more than half reporting that technology skills improved for a majority of students.

Although learning technology skills is secondary to subject-matter learning, the improvement in students' technology skills and in their ability to reason with information using an Internet-based assessment should not be considered a trivial or unintended benefit of participating in VHS. Many school principals expected that VHS would allow students in their schools to "learn how to learn" better in today's wired world. Students' increasing sophistication in using computers and the Web, combined with the increased capability of many of them to work independently in VHS courses, not only contributes to the fact that the teachers believe that the students are learning a lot, but also suggests that the students will be better prepared to learn in many unfamiliar settings, especially those in which use of the Internet is important. College is the most important new setting on the minds of many high school students and their parents, and college often does require greater independence and responsibility than high school. If VHS is able to help students "learn how to learn," particularly with technology, then, in the long term, many students will be able to apply their improved skills through online learning at college and in the workplace, where the Internet and the World Wide Web are increasingly common sources of both information and training. Even among the small minority of students who were not happy with VHS, there is appreciation of the value of the experience. One student wrote:

> I did not enjoy the VHS experience as a whole, but it was a good idea for me to take the class. Lots of colleges are using the Internet for instructional material, and I needed the experience of taking a class online.

No one is suggesting that learning from books or other nonelectronic sources is unimportant. Indeed, most VHS NetCourses require students to read books, which are shipped to the participating schools at the beginning of the semester. It is nonetheless significant that online courses help students to master a new information medium, the Internet.

Student Follow-Up Study

Another way to learn about the impact of VHS on its students is to ask them about their VHS experiences several years after they complete their courses. In the hope of speaking to many former participants about VHS, we selected two regular public schools, one in the Northeast and the other in the South, that had enrolled large numbers of students in VHS courses during the 1998–1999 academic year. Both were part of the Virtual High School program from its inception. With the help of school staff and parents, we were able to track down many of these former students. Out of a total group of 78 individuals, we were able to speak with 32 of them. Of those, 26 were in college, 3 were working, and 3 had just graduated from high school when we contacted them. Using a standardized interview protocol, we talked with each of these former VHS students for about 10 minutes. The 46 students with whom we did not speak could not be located or were not available.

Overall, from a vantage point several years later, most former students recalled VHS as an extremely positive experience. Nearly two-thirds of them reported that they were very satisfied with their VHS experience, and another quarter said that they were satisfied. Only 5 of the 32 former students reported being not very or not at all satisfied. Additional evidence of their satisfaction is demonstrated by the fact that a dozen of these individuals (nearly 40%) completed more than two VHS courses, including three who took four and one who took five NetCourses.

When asked what the best thing about the VHS program was, the most frequent responses identified working at one's own pace and taking a course that was not available otherwise at the regular school. The former students also realized that VHS required self-discipline and time-management skills, and many of them valued these aspects. One said, "It gave me more confidence with new experiences"; another said:

> It definitely prepares you to work more independently . . . and because the discussions cover so much and there is a lot of outside reading, it prepares you well for college in general. In particular, I took several classes from the University of Pennsylvania online, and the VHS experience prepared me for that wonderfully. I had no problems with that at all. In fact, I think in a lot of ways VHS was somewhat superior.

These comments reinforce the idea that students who are considering enrolling in any netcourse must realize that the online medium will provide them with a different experience from a face-to-face course. Virtual schools can offer courses not available in the regular high school, opportunities to interact with students from many different places, a more flexible schedule, and other advantages. At the same time, students should realize that they will need to be more independent and persistent than in face-to-face courses. More than half of VHS site coordinators reported that at least half the VHS students at their school had some type of difficulty communicating with a VHS teacher. Comparable data are not available for students in face-to-face courses, but it is certainly true that the online medium places special demands on teacher–student communication.

A number of the former students in the follow-up study identified specific knowledge or skills acquired through VHS that proved useful later. For example, a graphic artist thought that VHS had helped him improve his skills in working with computers, while an employee at a hospital said that VHS had piqued her interest in science. Another former VHS student reported studying literature that helped directly in later college studies. One young woman said, "Because of [the Model United Nations] course that I had taken, I had a better understanding of all the material that we were covering at the [Naval] Academy." Another respondent noted, "[The VHS course] improved my writing skills and my communication skills."

Responses such as those quoted above reinforce the teachers' and coordinators' opinions that many VHS students learn as much online as they do in regular courses. In addition, the online medium offers students certain advantages, such as more flexibility.

Students' Persistence and Grades in VHS Courses

At the same time that the Internet allows students to learn new subject matter and promotes the acquisition of certain information-processing skills, the use of the Internet by online schools also allows students new freedoms, such as the ability to "come to class" at any hour of the day or night. These new freedoms require that students take a greater degree of responsibility for independent work. Most VHS students have been able to handle these new freedoms and responsibilities well. However, it is important to examine dropout rates and grades for online courses because of the problems that arise when students do not properly handle their new responsibilities.

Dropouts. The problem of students' dropping out or not satisfactorily completing online courses is one that has been reported to be more prevalent than for similar face-to-face courses at all levels of education, not just for high school students. For example, the Florida Virtual School (FVS) evaluators report that in the 1999–2000 school year, 1,086 students enrolled in courses but never became active, and another 1,029 withdrew without a grade. This was in a year in which the student body "really consisted of 1,677 students who were actively involved in at least one course during the school year," meaning that the rate at which students "stopped out" or dropped out was indeed very high (Bigbie &

McCarroll, 2000, p. 180). Similarly, to take an example from the postsecondary level, among the several hundreds of thousands of students enrolled in distance education courses (including but not exclusively Internet-based) through the California community colleges system between 1995 and 2000, the completion rate for credit courses was only 52%, which was 13% lower than the rate for traditional courses (Hittelman, 2001). As reported in the same study, faculty believed that the most important barriers to the success of students in distance education courses were poor time-management skills, lack of self-motivation, and insufficient language skills. Females were reported to have slightly higher completion rates than males; similarly, Whites and Asian students had somewhat higher completion rates than African Americans, Hispanics, or Native Americans.

Defining who is a dropout is somewhat subjective in that different schools, whether online or face to face, will have different definitions of dropping out. FVS has a 28-day grace period after coursework begins, and students who leave during that time are not considered dropouts (Bigbie & McCarroll, 2000, p. 125). According to the FVS evaluation, the 1999–2000 dropout rate for the school was 8%. VHS began its operations with a short, 1-week drop period but after several years decided that 1 week was not long enough and extended the drop period to 5 weeks. For the 1999–2000 school year, using the 5-week drop period, VHS reported its dropout rate as 6%. Because so many students in both VHS and FVS are enrolled in a large number of face-to-face courses in addition to their netcourse, a student can often drop a netcourse without jeopardizing his or her academic program or status as a full-time student.

Grades. However, the situation is more complex and harder to interpret when we investigate students' grades. According to VHS records, for example, in one recent semester 1,541 student grades were awarded. A great many of the students did well in their courses, with more than half receiving an A or a B. But 244 students, or about 16%, received a failing grade, and another 8% received Ds. Thus, nearly one-quarter of the VHS grades were either Ds or Fs. That is an unusual distribution of grades, especially considering that many VHS students are college bound, take honors courses, and typically needed approval from their schools to enroll in an online course. These kinds of students don't usually get Ds and Fs in a quarter of their courses.

There are many possible explanations for these low grades. Perhaps VHS students' online courses are frequently "extra" courses that they don't need in order to graduate, and so they don't take those courses as seriously as they do their regular courses. Or certain courses might account for a large number of all the Ds and Fs, because these courses are low in quality or very difficult, or for some other reason. Then again, there may be a problem with the schools, some of which might do a worse job than others either in screening students who want to participate in VHS or in supporting students once they are selected, or both. Each of these possible explanations bears examination.

At the end of the semester in question, students were asked how the VHS course they were taking fit into their schedule. Only 13% indicated that the VHS course was part of their core program. Another 56% were taking a VHS course as an elective but still within the normal courseload (which varies for high school students, depending on state and local norms and even on their year in high school). Finally, for 31% of the students, the VHS course not only was an elective but also was being taken in addition to the normal courseload. The grades of students taking a VHS course in their core program consisted of 22% Ds and Fs. By comparison, the figures for students taking VHS as an elective within their normal courseload or in addition to it were 23% and 27%, respectively. It seems that the status of the course in the students' schedules does play some role in how well they do, albeit not a huge one.

With respect to the possible relationship between individual courses and low grades, only 10 VHS courses offered that semester had 50% or more Ds and Fs—a very high proportion of low grades. These 10 courses (about 8% of all the VHS courses that semester, responsible for awarding 6% of all grades) accounted for 54 of the Ds and Fs awarded that semester, or about 14%. Certainly, improving or eliminating these courses could help to reduce the proportion of Ds and Fs awarded. Yet, again, it would be hard to say that such an approach, by itself, would have a dramatic impact on the overall grading picture for VHS students.

The relationship between course quality and grades can be examined in another way, by looking at the students' ratings of the courses. As noted earlier, the great majority of students were satisfied with the quality of their courses. Among those who agreed that "the content in this course is of high quality," 23% received Ds or Fs in the course. By contrast, among students who did not believe the course was of high quality, 35% received Ds or Fs. Although one cannot say whether the poor grades led to a perception of poor quality or whether poor quality actually led to poor grades, there is an association between low ratings of course quality and poor grades. However, because there are not many courses that students find to be of low quality, as we already have concluded by using another approach, no dramatic change in grading can be accomplished solely by focusing on eliminating a few low-quality courses, whether the students' perceptions about quality are or are not accurate. Weeding out a few courses would have a marginal effect on the entire set of VHS grades.

One other hypothesis is that certain schools are at fault. Perhaps the site coordinators and guidance counselors in those schools were just not doing their job very well, allowing students to enter and complete VHS courses who should not have enrolled or who needed much more support than they actually received. Of the 174 schools enrolling students in VHS courses that semester, there were

19 in which more than two students had Ds or Fs and in which these low grades accounted for 50% or more of all the school's VHS grades that semester. This was about 11% of all the schools participating that semester, and yet the VHS students in those schools earned a total of 89 Ds and Fs, or about 24% of all the low grades. Putting it another way, if those 19 schools had not participated at all in VHS during that semester, the proportion of Ds and Fs awarded to students would have dropped from 24% to 20%, a distinct improvement. For whatever reasons—the guidance counselors, the site coordinators, the norms among the students, the technology infrastructure—some schools seem to be much less successful with online courses than others. The proportion of students earning Ds and Fs in those 19 schools was above 60%! This figure compares with 20% among the remaining schools.

Conclusions. Taken together, these separate perspectives on the problem of the many low grades suggests that this situation is too complex to allow for one easy explanation. Many factors contribute to the high proportion of students' VHS grades that are Ds and Fs (24%). For that reason, reducing the proportion of low grades is likely to be difficult and to require multiple actions. Course quality has to be rigorously reviewed and supported by VHS at all stages, in as many ways as possible. Students need to be carefully selected and then provided with both online and on-site assistance. Schools need to take the entire process seriously and monitor their students' experiences carefully. Taken together, there is a large set of "quality-control" procedures that need to be applied to virtual schools (these will be discussed in greater detail in Chapter 5). The same phenomenon appears at the postsecondary level. For example, in a study at Tidewater Community College (TCC) in Virginia (Tidewater Community College, 2001), if "success" is defined as earning a grade of A, B, or C, then the overall TCC success rate was 74%, compared to 61% for students in online courses and 92% for students in compressed video courses (a form of distance learning that is more similar to typical face-to-face coursework than to online schooling).

We conclude, on the basis of the data from both FVS and VHS, that large numbers of students either drop out of netcourses (meaning that they leave before the drop period ends) or "stop out" (by notifying the school that they are leaving the course after the drop period or by simply not doing much, if any, work in their netcourse). One VHS teacher said:

> Lots of students still do not understand the commitment it takes to successfully complete a VHS course. . . . Out of 20 students, I would estimate that during each semester, a little more than half do extremely well (A average) and the remainder drop the course, fail, or do very poorly. There are not many in the middle range.

This teacher's statistical data are badly skewed (as compared to VHS's actual experience overall), but the problem is nonetheless real. Another teacher said, "The biggest problem I had was determining at any given time who was in my course."

VHS has taken new steps to help site coordinators monitor students' grades. Teachers are now required to provide the cumulative grades of students in their NetCourse every 2 weeks, by entering them into an online database maintained by VHS. Both site coordinators and VHS central staff also have online access to that database, which allows them to become aware of students with low grades and take appropriate steps while there is still time for improvement. The intent of this system is to reduce the number of students awarded Ds and Fs. We will return to the topic of stopouts and dropouts in Chapter 5.

VHS's Impacts on Teachers

Learning to teach an online course is not easy, even for the best teachers. Teaching a VHS course is time-consuming, too; referring to the fall semester of school year 2000–2001, 89% of the teachers agreed that teaching and managing a VHS course is more time-consuming than a regular course, with more than half saying "a lot more" time-consuming. Despite these challenges, VHS has attracted an experienced and talented group of teachers. VHS is attractive to them for a number of reasons.

Learning more about the Internet and other technology, although a challenge, is appealing to many teachers. Because much of the software and many procedures used for teaching online were new to the participating teachers, more than 90% reported that they acquired new technology skills. VHS teachers, many of whom did *not* have any special skill with technology at the outset, sometimes became local computer gurus, providing help to other teachers in their departments. Often, such technological know-how transfers to regular courses, with teachers reporting that the ability to use a particular piece of software (e.g., HyperStudio) or hardware (e.g., a scanner) or to manage a variety of file formats was immediately useful in other courses and to help other teachers.

More than two-thirds of the teachers reported that VHS provided them with an opportunity to prepare and teach a course they had not taught before. Many of the teachers have a passion for the subject of the course they teach, and nearly 90% reported that their subject-matter knowledge increased as a result of their VHS work. In most cases, VHS provides the teachers with enough students to make it feasible to offer a course that often is too specialized to teach only in their home schools, thus opening up a teaching option not otherwise available.

In addition to learning about technology and about the subject they teach, more than 80% of the teachers said they acquired new teaching or assessment skills. Because the virtual classroom is so different from the face-to-face class-room, these new skills are necessary to be successful in the new medium. Three-quarters of the VHS teachers also reported that they were able to use new teaching or assessment skills in their regular, face-to-face courses.

High school teaching obviously involves a great deal of contact with ado-lescents, but when it comes to working closely with other adults, teaching can be a lonely profession. Nearly two-thirds of the VHS teachers reported that their interaction with teachers in other schools increased as a result of working in VHS. More than one in five of the teachers reported that such interactions in-creased "a lot." In a profession that is increasingly looking for ways to attract and retain talented people, many participating teachers find the opportunity of-fered by VHS to work with other teachers to be a significant one.

VHS teachers must balance the advantages of teaching in a virtual school with its disadvantages, such as the greater time that is needed by most teachers to teach an online course compared with one that is taught face to face. The bottom line is captured partly by expressions of teachers' overall satisfaction with VHS. In the fall 2000 semester, for example, more than half of the teachers reported that they were very satisfied with their experience, while only 3% reported being not at all or not very satisfied.

Outcomes for Administrators and Schools

Fewer than 5% of the school principals and district superintendents who had experience with VHS in the fall of 2000 reported that they were not satisfied with VHS. The main reason for administrators' satisfaction was that they felt that students were able to take courses that they otherwise would not have been able to take. Nearly half of the principals felt that the additional courses made available to students were "very important" to their schools. One principal re-ported that "many parents want [VHS] for their students." Her school board is also enthusiastic about VHS.

The original impetus for forming the Virtual High School—allowing schools to enlarge their course catalogs at relatively low cost—is, in effect, validated by the administrators. They are satisfied with the courses and services that have been offered through VHS and have been willing to pay for them. (And, as we have seen, the students agreed with the administrators, with two-thirds of them reporting that an important reason for taking a VHS course was that the subject wasn't available at their school.)

By providing high schools with courses they otherwise could not offer, VHS and other online schools are addressing an important need. The administra-tors at VHS schools believe that this need is being met and are satisfied with VHS's services.

Outcomes for Other Virtual Schools

When it comes time to compare outcomes of VHS with outcomes in other virtual high schools, the FVS evaluation apparently provides the data most comparable to those about VHS presented in this book. The findings of the FVS evaluators are similar in many important respects to those that have been presented
here about VHS. The fact that the findings are in agreement tends to increase
the credibility of both data sets.

FVS, like VHS, primarily serves students who take a single online course
at a time. However, although 51% of the FVS students during the 1999–2000
school year were public school students, the Florida school, unlike VHS, had
a large segment of students (42%) who were being home schooled. FVS has
had a very small minority population. "Customer satisfaction" in FVS has
been very high, as it has been for VHS. For example, 93% of district respondents said that the school benefited their district, 75% of parents believed that
students learned as much or more from the online courses as they did from
traditional high school courses, and 89% of the participating students (those
who completed or were in the process of completing an FVS course) reported
that the quality of their netcourses was as high or higher than that of regular
high school courses. The majority of participating FVS students (51%) would
recommend the school to other students, as would the majority of FVS parents
(91%).

Data about the "stopout" and dropout rates in FVS were presented earlier
in this chapter. The difficulty that many students have had completing FVS
courses led the evaluators to conclude that "the online environment may not be
for all learners, but it certainly fills a niche and should continue to provide
services to students across Florida" (Bigbie & McCarroll, 2000, p. 182).

The FVS evaluation presents data comparing participating students with
noncompleters in terms of their ratings of student–teacher communication. Although the majority in both groups rated communication as "good," the noncompleters reported communication as poor or fair (38% in all) more often than the
participating students (16%). For VHS students, a similar finding is that 84%
of students who received As or Bs agreed that "the teacher frequently communicates with me," while only about 64% of the students who received Ds or Fs
agreed with this statement. In both online schools, there is a strong suggestion
that communication difficulties may be one of the major factors contributing to
the high stopout and dropout rates observed in online high school courses. However, notwithstanding the large number of students who stop out of the FVS
courses, most students who do complete the courses receive an A or a B and
report, as previously noted, that they learn as much or more than in face-to-face
courses.

Conclusions

A large majority of students, teachers, site coordinators, and administrators find the VHS program valuable and are satisfied with the services that it provides. The most important benefit provided by VHS is offering access to courses that otherwise would not be available. Furthermore, there is a documented need for many high schools to expand their catalogs. For example, a recent report of the Commission on the Future of the Advanced Placement Program (2001) notes that "43% of American high schools do not offer AP courses, and many participating schools offer only a few courses." The report specifically recommends expanding AP access in underserved schools. Many administrators see a need to expand other offerings in their high schools, too, not just AP courses.

Although the evidence is incomplete, it appears that students who complete virtual courses learn as much from the courses they study online as their counterparts do in face-to-face courses. In addition, students seem to learn more information-management and technology skills in online courses than they do in face-to-face courses, although again the evidence is incomplete.

VHS teachers also benefit from participating. They obtain access to new technologies, learn technology skills, and bring these skills to their other courses. Also, a large majority of the VHS teachers are able to teach a course that they want to teach but probably could not teach in a face-to-face setting because the enrollments would be low.

Although VHS and other online schools offer real benefits (mainly allowing students to learn material in courses not otherwise available to them), there are certain problems as well. Some types of courses, such as those that require close physical inspection of objects while engaged in discussions with other students or the teacher, do not appear to work as well online as others. Also—as is true in postsecondary distance education courses—a significant fraction of students do not do as well online as others, either not persisting long enough to be graded or persisting but getting poor grades. Related to that finding, some regular high schools seem not to do as well supporting students in virtual courses as others.

An evaluation of Florida's online high school provides confirmation of many important findings about VHS's outcomes. That the evaluations are independent, and that they examined related efforts but in different places and with different participants, adds weight to the conclusions of both studies.

Chapter 5

LESSONS LEARNED

The experience of the Virtual High School teaches many lessons about what an online high school can and cannot do. VHS has already provided thousands of students with courses that are highly rated by many people, including outside reviewers. It has energized hundreds of fine teachers, taught them new skills, and made it possible for their expertise to be more widely shared. VHS has made its way into schools in communities in half of the states, and it has transitioned from a federal demonstration project to become an independent nonprofit organization. In short, VHS has accomplished a great deal in 5 years.

And yet, in spite of the fact that the designers of LearningSpace thoughtfully used familiar features to organize the online "classroom," it is apparent that interactions in virtual classes are not the same, in many important respects, as those in face-to-face classes. Although it is fair to say that netcourses have unique strengths, they also have serious weaknesses. As remarkable as current Internet technologies are, their shortcomings are one contributor to the weaknesses of netcourses. A second area of weakness is that netcourses work best for independent learners. Although participating in a netcourse may help to develop more autonomy and responsibility in some students, it is clear that for many more students the supports are simply not enough to induce them to persist and succeed in the online environment. Another weakness is that the need in certain classes for direct interactions with people or objects (such as science laboratory equipment) is not successfully reproduced in netcourses—and may never be. For these and perhaps for other reasons, neither VHS nor any other virtual school has proved a success for all of the students who have enrolled; indeed, so far as one can tell from available data, virtual schools do not succeed for as high a percentage of comparable students who are enrolled in similar face-to-face courses.

In considering the lessons learned from VHS, it is important to keep in mind both its successes and its shortcomings—what it has accomplished and what it has not been able to accomplish. This chapter begins with lessons learned by focusing on some of the components that are distinctive to VHS, including the consortium model, the use of site coordinators, the development of the Teachers Learning Conference (TLC), and the adoption of the LearningSpace technology. As we have seen, many virtual schools share common features, and it is not claimed that each of these particular components is unique to VHS. However, these components are important to VHS, they represent choices that distinguish it from many other virtual schools, and there are important lessons to be learned about each of them.

Other lessons are more generic; they grow out of experiences that seem likely to be common to all virtual high schools. The topics of these lessons include an assessment of what it takes for students and teachers to be successful in an online environment, the nature of quality control for netcourses, the need for high standards and for a kind of "truth in advertising" for virtual schools, and consideration of the ways in which technology is and is not able to bring about changes in high schools. After considering such a wide variety of lessons in this chapter, the focus in the next and final chapter turns to the future of virtual schools.

Lessons from VHS

The designers of VHS had a multitude of choices to make as they began to sketch their proposal on paper in 1996. After 5 years, many of the key choices remain unchanged, reflecting the confidence of the VHS staff that the original decisions are still sound.

Consortium Model

As pointed out in Chapter 2, the consortium model is an unusual one for virtual schools. Especially at this early stage in the development of virtual schooling, there is room for many approaches. However, it is clear that the consortium model used by VHS has many strengths.

Tinkering with the Existing "School Grammar." As we noted in Chapter 1, Tyack and Cuban's book (1995) offers important clues about which kinds of school reforms survive and which do not. The VHS model enlists the support and skills of teachers as key actors in reform, and it also provides local administrators with opportunities to define problems and devise solutions (for example, by allowing certain VHS courses to be offered for credit but not others). The local variations observed in VHS (with regard to the role of the site coordinator, the ways in which the students are selected, the number of VHS teachers at the school, the times and places that VHS students meet face to face with their site coordinator and with other VHS students at their school, etc.) should not be viewed as mere footnotes to the VHS model. Rather, according to Tyack and Cuban's way of thinking, successful change models *must* allow for creative "tinkering" and local adaptations.

Successful innovations, then, may have certain startling new characteristics and yet, at the same time, need to fit with the existing "school grammar," as well as with local needs. Although the idea of students taking a netcourse taught from hundreds or thousands of miles away is in some respects a radical departure from current practice—as is the notion of students' possibly "coming to class" in their pajamas—much of the success of the VHS model depends on the fact that so many components of VHS are already familiar to its participants. At the same time that VHS challenges creative people to master the new skills and new ways of thinking that are required to design, offer, support, and succeed in netcourses, it offers them the knowledge that most of the teachers' and students' time will continue to be spent in face-to-face courses, as usual. In this respect, particularly, it seems fair to say that the netcourses are "tinkering" with a standard structure of schooling that in most respects remains unchanged.

Approaching the same idea from a different direction, one of the most important strengths of the consortium approach is that it allows current teachers to build and deliver their own new courses. This possibility seems to unlock a passionate commitment on the part of VHS teachers to assure the success of *their* VHS courses and *their* online students. Although the resulting VHS catalog is eclectic, the courses appeal to and meet the needs of administrators and students in hundreds of schools. The quality of the courses is high, despite the fact that the teachers must work harder to teach an online course than a regular course. Teachers who have been encouraged to be creative, in an environment that has strong quality controls in place, have been able to deliver interesting and effective instruction through the Internet. The actions of these teachers qualify as another form of "creative tinkering" within the standard model of the American high school.

There are other values to the consortium approach as well. The enormous number of course offerings in the VHS catalog is far easier to achieve when the challenge of creating the courses is shared across many institutions. The cost of participating in VHS is reduced by the implicit barter of teachers' services among schools. The individuals in the participating schools also believe, for good reason, that they are helping to build something new, not just acting as "consumers," and this belief is a motivating factor for many of them.

Problematic Features of the Model. However, there are also features of the VHS model that are problematic. One of the notable disadvantages of using a national approach that relies on participating schools' schedules, as VHS does, is that the annual school calendar varies greatly from one state and region to another. Some schools, such as many in Georgia, begin in August, well before Labor Day. Other schools, such as in the Northeast, begin weeks later. Therefore, VHS has had to contend with students who enroll in the same VHS course but whose schedules at the beginning and end of semesters vary by as much as 3 weeks. To provide for these differences in the calendar, VHS asks teachers to create 3-week-long modules that students can complete at the beginning or end of their course and that do not depend on having all enrolled students participate simultaneously. This is an unusual feature of the VHS courses, at least as compared with most face-to-face courses. The variety of school calendars also creates some difficulty in providing interim and final grades to students' schools on a schedule that meets the requirements of school calendars in different states and regions. Although very few of the VHS teachers reported that differences in the students' school calendars caused major difficulties, about half (51%) did report moderate difficulties. It is more challenging for some courses than for others to integrate the 3-week-long modules, and site coordinators also vary in the degree to which they communicate with students about the demands of the VHS schedule.

Conclusions. As VHS has evolved and expanded over the years, it has increasingly allowed schools to participate that do not contribute a teacher or a VHS course. In this respect, although it is still primarily a consortium in which participating schools both offer and receive courses, the VHS model has become somewhat diluted from the original vision.

Nonetheless, the consortium approach remains both a hallmark of VHS and one of its great strengths. We have learned again the appeal of a reform that permits and encourages local involvement and local variation. Tyack and Cuban's notion of "creative tinkering" within a framework of well-accepted structures is consistent with the VHS model and helps to explain its accomplishments to date. Creating a successful "collaboration model" was one of VHS's original goals, and using this model has proved to be a particularly important and successful part of the VHS experience.

Preparing Teachers for Online Teaching

If the participation of teachers from schools all over the country is one of the greatest strengths of VHS, then the training that they receive seems to be one of the vital reasons why they are able to successfully design and teach high-quality NetCourses. The online graduate-level course taken by each new VHS teacher serves many functions, providing them with nuts-and-bolts information about using an unfamiliar piece of software, illuminating the idea that the facilitation of students' work (rather than direct instruction) is often more important in a NetCourse than in a face-to-face course, guiding teachers in developing a new syllabus, and directing teachers to use certain standard approaches and elements in their work with students (such as carefully introducing students to the on-screen "buttons"—such as the button to access the CourseRoom—that appear throughout a NetCourse and that are illustrated in several figures in Chapter 3), to name a few.

The teachers agree that the TLC has been effective. Among the teachers who taught a VHS course during the 2000–2001 school year, more than two-thirds reported that the professional development NetCourse in which they participated—either the TLC or NetCourse Instructional Methodologies (NIM)—was very effective in helping them to implement a VHS course. Only about 3% felt that their preparation was not very or not at all effective. Teachers also were positive about many specific aspects of their preparation in the TLC or the NIM, such as learning to use the technology effectively and learning how to include opportunities for student-to-student interaction in a VHS course. However, despite the persistent efforts of members of the VHS central staff, teachers still reported that it was difficult to incorporate successful large- or small-group activities in VHS courses. Only about one-third of teachers reported that their preparation was very effective in helping them do this.

Teachers also continued to request and receive assistance from members of the central staff after completing the TLC or NIM training. For example, more than half have asked for assistance in using administrative software (e.g., to report students' grades), and nearly 90% requested help in using Learning-Space. The great majority of teachers who asked for assistance received it and found that it was helpful to them.

Tracy Sheehan enrolled in the TLC in 1997. Members of her particular online discussion group in the TLC were very active and averaged about 30 postings apiece. Sheehan was one of the least active members of the group, in terms of the frequency of online postings. Several months into the TLC, in the spring, she was still struggling, writing that "Overwhelmed is putting it mildly. Of course, I made my own problems with starting slow and thinking I would have more time. I am still lost on some things but maybe with a little help from my friends I can finish catching up." Sheehan did an extraordinary amount of work during the summer, after the TLC ended, and did manage to catch up. In spite of her slow start, she thought that the TLC was useful.

Through VHS, we have learned that online teaching is challenging, it is not for everyone, and it requires careful preparation. In the presence of good preparation through the TLC and the NIM, hundreds of teachers, many of whom did not begin as experts in technology, have learned to become successful Net-Course instructors. As noted in Chapter 1, one of VHS's explicit goals was to create a successful network-based professional development course for teachers. Not only has VHS succeeded in meeting this goal, the importance of the goal has been clearly demonstrated.

Site Coordinators

Just as teaching through the Internet is not an intuitive idea for many people, creating the job of the site coordinator—a feature of VHS that was included in the original 1996 Challenge Grant proposal—is not necessarily an obvious choice. Many virtual schools began without the equivalent of site coordinators.

Although the value of having someone at each school to help VHS students is easy to understand, there are also significant costs associated with providing such help. And if the site coordinators are specially trained, as they are in VHS, there are added training costs. These various costs make the question of whether the site coordinators are "worth it" an important one to ask.

Administrators' Opinions. Principals of the schools participating in VHS during 2000–2001 were asked that question. The survey item noted that "students in VHS courses must have both a VHS teacher *and* a VHS coordinator," and asked whether the additional resources were justified and acceptable. A majority of the principals (62%) answered yes, while only 14% answered no, and the remaining 24% were not sure. A follow-up question asked whether the principals would pay a $6,000 fee to VHS, as well as paying the in-school expenses of the VHS teacher and site coordinator, and 51% answered that they would definitely (14%) or probably (37%) pay these fees. Many district superintendents also understand that the coordinator is important. One said, when asked about possible changes to VHS, "Keep the coordinators; that role is key."

Teachers' and Students' Opinions. During the first several years of VHS's operation, as roles and responsibilities of all participants became clearer and better defined, the teachers became increasingly supportive of the site coordinators. By the 1999–2000 school year, when the VHS teachers were asked whether the role of VHS site coordinator should be continued, more than three-fourths of the respondents (77%) agreed that it should, and another 18% indicated that the role should continue with some modifications. Only 5% of the teachers did not want to have site coordinators at all. Teachers' comments included these:

> VHS site coordinators are vital to the continued success of the long distance learning program. [Our site coordinator] has been of significant importance to both the VHS students and myself in assisting with the on site management of the VHS program.

> I cannot imagine what a school would do without a site coordinator. The role is crucial to the success of the program. The site coordinator is responsible for the students, computers, communication, organization, etc.

> Most of the problems I have in the day-to-day operation of my own class result from site coordinators who do not do their job.

Statistics have already been cited in Chapter 2 showing that the students are aware of many of the functions that site coordinators perform. The students also value the role of the coordinators, with 88% agreeing that the coordinator was able to assist them with technical problems and 40% agreeing that the coordinator "helped me stay on schedule and make progress in my VHS course."

Costs and Conclusions. The participants clearly are in favor of maintaining the site coordinator's role. If the VHS model were very different—for example, if only a tiny handful of students in a school were enrolled in NetCourses—the site coordinator's role might be less important. Certainly, the cost would have to be reduced in that case, and perhaps someone could play the coordinator's role on top of his or her regular duties in the high school. However, enrollments in VHS schools are distributed in blocks of 10 or 20 students, and it is difficult to imagine not providing on-site support to that many students, particularly if, as is likely to be the case for years to come, none of the students, or at most very few of them, have had prior experience taking a NetCourse.

The cost of the site coordinators in the VHS model still looms as an unsettled issue. The original VHS proposal was less than clear about these costs over the long term. The goals of the VHS project described in that proposal (and listed in Chapter 1) do not mention the site coordinators. Indeed, the goal of creating a collaborative that will "share resources" tends to focus attention on the implicit exchange of one section of a teacher's time for the benefit of enrolling approximately one section of students in other schools' NetCourses—a viewpoint in which the coordinator's role is missing from the financial equation. The question of whether VHS is meeting its goal of creating "a collaboration model that is feasible for all schools, scalable, and replicable" includes the vital subquestion of whether the cost structure is "feasible for all schools." This is a question to which we will return in Chapter 6. Setting aside the difficult question of cost for the time being makes it much easier to gauge the value of the site coordinators.

It is clear that students enrolled in netcourses have fewer familiar supports than they do in face-to-face courses. For example, a teacher can more easily locate and talk to a student who is falling behind or having difficulty in a face-to-face course than track down a student hundreds of miles away who has not contributed to a netcourse. The teacher may not even know whether the student is truly absent or is "lurking" online. In this environment, we have learned that site coordinators play an important role in providing the new kind of supports that netcourses require, and we know that students, teachers, and other participants value their work.

LearningSpace Technology

As mentioned in Chapter 3, the LearningSpace technology shaped the VHS experience in specific ways. It clearly provided a degree of flexibility that is normally not available in traditional high school courses. Both VHS teachers and students expressed satisfaction with the ability to teach or take their course at home and at times that suited their needs. As with other online environments, the LearningSpace user interface capitalized on everyday features of schools and classrooms—features such as the Schedule, the MediaCenter, and the CourseRoom—to make the software easy for students to use. The way the course is structured by the LearningSpace environment focuses teachers toward communication with individual students, rather than the whole-class communication more typical of a face-to-face class. Even when the teacher is engaged in a discussion with the whole class, his or her comments are often a reply to the comments of an individual student. As a result, VHS students expressed a high degree of satisfaction about the nature of communications with their teachers, even though some students were concerned about the amount of time it took for teachers to respond to their questions. (Private messages between teacher and student are also supported.)

Limitations. On the other hand, there also were some important limitations in the LearningSpace environment. Some of these limitations were self-imposed. For example, to enable teachers to maintain control over student discourse in their virtual classrooms, the VHS central administration turned off the capability in LearningSpace for students to start discussions. Teachers, however, could choose to give students this privilege in their particular course. Another self-imposed limitation was on the amount of multimedia that was available to students in the MediaCenter. Teachers had the capability of posting a wide variety of pictures and other media material. But when students were asked about the MediaCenter, a large majority of them said that it did not include audio or video clips for their courses. The dominant medium in VHS courses is still text.

Other limitations were imposed by the technology and its design. Some of these same, user-friendly, everyday classroom features made it more difficult for teachers and students to do what they wanted to do and limited the pedagogical innovativeness of the experience. By defining the otherwise limitless electronic boundaries as the "space" of a classroom of enrolled students (e.g., restricting course participants to those specifically enrolled as VHS students), Learning-Space made it difficult for Terry Haugen to include teachers and students from the Ukraine in her Russian studies course. Likewise, Anita Bergh was not able to teach her poetry class in collaboration with a community college, because those additional people she would have wanted as participants were not students registered for her course.

Although teachers had (but did not often use) access to a range of media for their presentations, it was more difficult for students to submit their assignments in a variety of media forms. This can be a serious limitation to constructivist pedagogy in the age of multimedia. This limitation was particularly significant in certain types of courses, such as hands-on courses, where laboratories are used.

The asynchronous nature of communication in LearningSpace affected student collaboration, student–student communication, and the timeliness of teacher responses. In surveys and interviews of teachers, coordinators, and students, we found that group work and interaction in VHS courses were less satisfactory than in regular courses. As Tracy Sheehan put it, "Teamwork, on the other hand, is easier in the classroom. Kids [in her VHS course] have more trouble getting into the team; they aren't in the same week." Several teachers and students in our interviews expressed the need for at least occasional synchronous chat.

Synchronous Communication. The issue of synchronous versus asynchronous communication is a real tension within VHS. Actually, the version of LearningSpace that VHS chose to use (version 3.5) is not the most current. Later versions of LearningSpace have synchronous chat, and the most recent version at this writing (version 5) has the capability of live videoconferencing. VHS adopted version 3.5 because it had some important capabilities that were discontinued in version 4, and version 5 was still being tested at the time. But the VHS staff members have strong reservations about the use of synchronous communications. They believe that asynchronous discussion allows for reflective postings that synchronous discussion does not. The use of synchronous communications also works against the "any time" effect that they are trying to achieve. Some students agree with this view. For example, one student stated, "It would be lovely to have everyone on at the same time, but the whole point of taking a class online, for me, was to be able to work with people that don't live in my stupid little town. That comes at a price and the price is that we don't all work on the same time schedule." Nonetheless, other students felt that even 1 hour a week of synchronous communication would enrich their experience and help their collaboration. And synchronous communication need not involve the entire class at once; it might involve as few as two people, such as a teacher helping a student or one classmate collaborating with another.

Conclusions. Despite some of the limitations of LearningSpace, and sometimes because of its capabilities, many VHS teachers were able to create satisfying and effective virtual learning experiences for their students. A key is maintaining student engagement in an asynchronous environment. Tracy Sheehan suggests, "For VHS, a lot of small assignments do better than a few large ones. Don't do the whole big thing all at once." Here she echoes Anita Bergh, who also used many small assignments to maintain student engagement in her poetry course. Also, teachers need to interact regularly with students. As Tracy

Sheehan put it, "I check on my students daily." VHS's Liz Pape also emphasizes the importance of this:

> The way we are working to address student frustration over wait-time for teacher responses is to address teacher presence in the CourseRoom. We are more closely monitoring how often teachers are in the CourseRoom and are more quickly reminding the non-shows that they are in noncompliance of the VHS attendance policy. If a teacher doesn't attend a CourseRoom, chat will not provide the solution. Synchronous or asynchronous, if no one is there to answer the call, the frustration will still be there.

Lessons About Virtual Schooling

Particular choices made by VHS or any other virtual school are important—be they choices about the nature of the course catalog, the technology used to deliver courses, the background and training of the teachers, or other elements of online schooling. However, there is a set of issues that, at least in this early stage of the development of virtual schools, seem to transcend particular details and that speak instead to the very nature of this new approach to teaching and delivering courses. Although these issues can be examined from the perspective of VHS, in all likelihood the same issues could be explored from the perspective of the Florida Virtual School or any virtual school. Four such issues are discussed below.

Who Succeeds in Online Schools?

It has become apparent that there are teachers and students who will not flourish in virtual courses. Working in this new medium requires highly motivated people who are willing and able to master new skills. The fact that a teacher is effective in face-to-face courses does not mean that he or she will be effective in an online environment. Similarly, for students it is not simply a matter of predicting that students who have earned good grades in regular courses will succeed online. It doesn't always work that way. Some students who are not high achievers in regular classrooms become highly motivated and do well in a netcourse, whereas some high-achieving students seem to lose their focus and commitment when working online. One VHS teacher said, "Most kids are capable of doing the work in this course, but it requires independence and responsibility." He added that he had a student who was in special education in her regular school who successfully completed his VHS course. Although he knew that her progress was slow, "I didn't even know she was in special ed until the last session."

VHS posts an online form, the Student Pre-Enrollment Questionnaire, that prospective students are encouraged to complete. The idea is that a student's score (which is provided online at the push of a button after answering the questions) is a good indicator of whether or not he or she is a good candidate for enrolling in a netcourse. The 15 questions focus on such topics as the degree to which students are willing to take responsibility for their own learning, whether or not they usually do their work on time, and their reading and writing abilities. A companion document explains the thinking behind each of the questions. For example, questions about prospective students' reading abilities are explained with the comment that "most of the content of VHS courses is text based," strongly suggesting that poor readers need to think twice before enrolling in a typical netcourse.

Using this online questionnaire to help prospective students screen themselves is a good idea, and it is no doubt a useful activity for some of them. Nonetheless, the high proportion of Ds and Fs earned by VHS students, as discussed in Chapter 4, demonstrates that the current system for selecting or screening VHS students still needs improvement. A number of the VHS teachers commented on how important it is that students who want to be enrolled in a VHS course be clear about what is demanded and be discouraged from enrolling if they are unclear.

VHS is by no means the only virtual school to experience dropout or "stopout" problems. The experience of the Florida Virtual School (FVS) is similar. Even with a 4-week drop period, for every 100 students who began a course in 1999–2000, 26 had dropped out by end of the school year and another 8 were still working toward completing the course. In light of these data, and given the large number of additional students who enrolled but then did not become active or who withdrew within the 4-week drop period, the FVS evaluators recommended that the school "continue to closely track status data, especially of non-completers, and use the information to influence policy and processes in the future" (Bigbie & McCarroll, 2000). Both VHS and FVS are aware that one source of the dropout problem is that some high school students procrastinate and fail to hand in work that is due, eventually reaching a point where it is nearly impossible for them to complete the course and get a good grade. In the case of FVS, according to the November 2000 evaluation report, more than 20% of its students were in the ninth grade (meaning they were only about 15 years old) and their dropout rate was a remarkable 39%. Many students at this age lack the independence and discipline needed to succeed in an online course.

Another school, Apex, which has raised tens of millions of dollars from private investors, also experienced a dropout problem from its advanced placement (AP) courses during the 1999–2000 school year. Of the 600 students in

28 states who took AP courses from Apex that year, the *New York Times* reported that two-thirds did not complete sufficient work to take a final examination (Steinberg, 2000). The article quoted one student as saying, "I didn't feel like doing any work. I'm just not organized a lot of the time." One of Apex's responses to the high dropout rate was to provide training for "mentor teachers" in the schools, who were to play a role similar to VHS's site coordinators.

Although virtual high schools are still in their infancy, we have learned that a high proportion of students who enroll in online courses drop out or earn poor grades. Continuing efforts need to be made to screen prospective students carefully, counseling out those who seem unlikely to succeed. Parents, guidance counselors, site coordinators, principals, and others with a stake in virtual high schools need to be aware of the dropout problem.

Virtual high schools, such as VHS and FVS, that allow data about students' experiences to be published should be commended for their openness. State school boards, chief state school officers, and the public should insist that more virtual high schools provide useful data about students' experiences, including the dropout rates and the percentages of students earning good grades (As, Bs, or Cs) or poor grades (Ds or Fs). The best situation would be to publish such data by course, but publishing data for a semester's or a year's worth of courses would be a good start.

The fact that many students find it challenging to persist and do well in netcourses in which they have chosen to enroll relates to one of the goals that VHS set for itself at the outset. VHS set out to "serve a diverse group of students." How one chooses to define "diverse" influences the degree to which one judges whether this goal has been met. But it is clear that students must have a higher-than-average degree of motivation to succeed in online courses, and for VHS this has meant serving many more honors and college-bound students than others.

Nonetheless, we should not lose sight of the fact that thousands of high school students are doing well in online courses and are learning a great deal. We turn next to the question of what has been learned about controlling the quality of virtual schools.

The Importance of Quality Control

A wide variety of people, skills, and procedures are needed to make an online school work. As with any complex undertaking, it is difficult to point to one person, one component, or one approach that is the single most important element. Although the quality of the teachers would certainly be a strong candidate for the "most important" component, the technology, the site coordinators, the guidance counselors, and the central administrative staff all play other critical roles.

Perhaps it is the very fact that there is no single key to success for virtual schools that leads to one of the most interesting lessons. More than in face-to-face schools and classrooms, where so many procedures have become routine, online schools require attention to a large number of features and details that, for the moment, are far from routine. These features or components range, as we have seen, from choices about what technologies to use, to procedures for choosing and preparing students and teachers, to the selection of courses to include in the catalog. Some decisions that may seem to be of relatively minor consequence—the length of the add/drop period, the timetable for reporting students' grades to participating schools, methods for adjudicating disputes—can turn out to be anything but minor, affecting participants' morale, the reputations of the school and its staff, and ultimately the viability of the whole enterprise. For virtual schools, "the devil is in the details."

For example, a primary goal of any virtual high school is to offer net-courses of high quality. However, it is not enough simply to identify the elements that lead to quality and then hope that dozens and dozens of courses will be excellent just because teachers are implored to do a good job. As virtual schools grow, it is essential that they have a variety of more formal quality-control mechanisms in place.

In other words, if there is any secret to effective quality control of net-courses, it seems to be to focus on quality at every stage, from selection of the teachers through ongoing examination of the courses as they are delivered to students. This thoroughness means that quality control is expensive. On the other hand, without effective quality control, serious questions about virtual high school providers are very likely to be raised. As one participant said, "Without quality control, they don't have a real virtual high school."

Quality-Control Procedures. It is not difficult to identify at least 10 quality-control procedures used by VHS, and the list could easily be extended. These procedures include:

- *Selection of teachers.* As has been pointed out, teaching an online course is not for everyone—not even for all teachers who are known to be effective in a face-to-face environment. For example, a teacher who is an inspiring performer in person may not organize materials well or be skilled at facilitating student discussions. From the first year, VHS has proved adept at selecting teachers who do well in an online environment. Becoming an excellent VHS teacher requires working hard to master a new medium.
- *Professional development for teachers.* Enrollment in the TLC is a requirement for all new VHS teachers, except that some teachers now enroll in a variant of the TLC, NetCourse Instructional Methodologies (NIM), that focuses on teaching a section of a NetCourse that has already been developed. The TLC is a

26-week online professional development course for prospective VHS teachers. By becoming students in the medium, these teachers learn firsthand what their students will face. Experienced online instructors offer information and assistance on a wide variety of topics that are essential to online teaching.

- *The use of written standards of quality.* Prospective VHS teachers are introduced to quality standards during the TLC or the NIM. They rapidly learn that VHS staff will be examining the course materials and syllabi that they develop to be sure that the materials conform with the written standards of quality. The standards cover everything from the way that the teachers use fonts and colors to present themselves online to the nature of the course content and the way that it is organized in LearningSpace. By now, several key organizations have promulgated standards and/or policies related to high school NetCourses, but VHS was among the first to develop them. The next section in this chapter describes the standards in greater detail.

- *Reviews of online courses prior to their first offering.* One goal of the TLC is to help prospective VHS teachers develop NetCourses that they will teach. Although a NetCourse is not typically completely finished by the end of the TLC, VHS instructors and staff review it carefully. If too little progress has been made or if the course does not meet quality-control standards, it will not be part of the VHS course catalog. Each year, some number of developing NetCourses are not ready to be included in VHS.

- *"Testing" of prospective VHS teachers.* Instructors in the TLC have an opportunity to observe the prospective VHS teachers interacting with their colleagues and with the instructors. Individuals who don't learn how to use the online medium or the LearningSpace technology effectively enough to persuade the instructors that they will be good VHS teachers will "wash out." As the years have gone by, members of the VHS staff have developed an increasingly well-honed sense of what it takes to be a successful online teacher.

- *Faculty advisors.* From the outset, with access to all the password-protected sites, VHS staff used LearningSpace technology to observe NetCourses in action. It is possible to do the equivalent of a classroom observation by monitoring the teacher's and the students' postings. Staff members look for such basic elements as whether the teacher is providing regular feedback to students at least several times each week (and preferably daily) and for such subtle elements as whether the course material is being explained well and mastered by students at an appropriate pace. As the number of VHS courses grew, it became apparent that the staff could not effectively monitor all the NetCourses. A set of new positions was created for faculty advisors. These advisors serve somewhat the same role as department chairs in high schools, with particular emphasis on being sure that the NetCourses in a given field (mathematics, say) are of high quality. But unlike regular high schools, VHS requires multiple faculty advisors in any given discipline, so that the hundreds of VHS course offerings can be effectively monitored. The faculty advisors are paid to provide regular feedback to VHS teachers, especially first-time teachers, based on observations of their NetCourses as they are being offered.

- *Training and use of site coordinators.* The role of the site coordinator has already been discussed. Like the VHS teachers, new site coordinators are required to take an online course that helps prepare them for their new responsibilities. By acting as advisors and advocates for students and as local partners for the remote VHS teachers, the coordinators can solve problems that otherwise might become more serious. The quality of students' experiences is related, in part, to the presence of the site coordinators.
- *Student surveys.* Near the end of every semester, VHS puts a survey online for students to complete. The resulting data are analyzed in part to identify courses that are perceived by students as weak in one way or another.
- *Written agreements with schools.* VHS requires that schools satisfy certain minimum requirements, such as having appropriate technology in place for students to use when they take the VHS courses. Putting the agreements in writing, and insisting that they be signed by the district's superintendent, suggests that the agreements are important. Besides promising to have in place the minimum technology requirements, participating schools need to agree to a variety of other conditions, such as to provide 20% release time for a local VHS site coordinator, pay for the VHS teacher and site coordinator to participate in VHS's online training courses, pay for books or other materials that students in other schools are required to use for the NetCourse taught by the VHS teacher at this school, and returning to VHS at the end of each semester all materials and books that have been sent to the school and used by VHS students for NetCourses they have taken during that semester.
- *Parental notification.* If students are doing poorly, VHS notifies the parents that there is a problem. Procedures also are in place for reporting midterm grades and for reporting and resolving problems. (Note that parents are not able to monitor their child's online VHS work—nor do they routinely interact with the VHS teacher—which makes it more important, if a student is doing poorly, to involve the site coordinator in the local school as well as to notify the parents.)

To summarize, we have learned that few procedures can be taken for granted in online schools. Excellence, where and when it occurs, is the result of a large number of well-conceived, well-staffed, and well-conducted activities. Establishing standards to help assure that these efforts result in online learning experiences of high quality is the topic of the next section.

Standards for Online Courses

Since 1989, enormous effort has been focused on improving American elementary and secondary education through the development and application of education standards. The first set of national content standards for grades K–12 were published in that year by the National Council of Teachers of Mathematics. In the years since, standards-based education reform has been on the agendas of presidents, governors, school boards, and others. The focus on standards has many meanings and interpretations, focusing on what is taught, on how learning and teaching are organized, and even on the assessment of students' learning.

The Purposes of Standards. Beginning in 1996, various organizations have tried to establish standards for Internet-based courses and programs. Much of this work has been aimed at higher education because distance education through the Internet has spread so much more quickly through institutions of higher education than through secondary schools. However, interest in establishing standards for Internet-based courses for high schools has also emerged. In either case, for secondary or postsecondary education, organizations are trying to develop principles of practice to help both developers and students understand what makes for a high-quality online experience. Once such an understanding is reached, people can act. There are already some pertinent legal standards in place; for example, the U.S. Department of Education's student loan program sets a lower limit of 50% on the fraction of time that students must be engaged in face-to-face instruction to be eligible for loans. However, the organizations working on standards—including the National Education Association, the American Federation of Teachers, and the Southern Regional Education Board—are first of all trying to structure and disseminate knowledge about the principles or standards that underlie good practice for netcourses, not laws or regulations. Other institutions, such as colleges and universities, are then free to set requirements based on the standards being disseminated nationwide, if they want to do so.

In addition, VHS has established certain standards for its own internal use. For example, the TLC instructors have developed a lengthy set of "TLC Evaluation Criteria," which apply to VHS courses that are under development. At one point, the list included 129 criteria, focusing on the organization of course materials, the use of LearningSpace features, communication of course expectations and policies, and other topics. Criteria, or standards, ranged from expectations about the font sizes to be used in LearningSpace to the frequency of grading students' work to the nature of the syllabus. Because the TLC is an "incubator" for new courses, the TLC instructors have a golden opportunity not only to explain what makes for good practice but to insist on revisions to course materials if these standards are not being met.

VHS also commissioned two external groups to develop standards for netcourses. One of these, the Netcourse Evaluation Board (on which the SRI evaluation staff was represented), developed Instructional Standards, relating to the content and pedagogy of the netcourses themselves, and Operational Standards, relating to the delivery of the courses (e.g., specifying the technology available to students; the supports at the school, such as site coordinators; and other aspects of the delivery system). VHS makes use of these standards with teachers, and they were also important as a starting point for other sets of standards, including those developed by the SRI expert panel, shown in Chapter 3, Figure 3.2.

Promoting Standards Useful for High School Netcourses. One important group with a member on the Netcourse Evaluation Board was the National Education Association (NEA), an organization that represents more than 2 million teachers and other staff in schools, colleges, and universities. Soon after the Netcourse Evaluation Board established its standards in 1999, the NEA issued a Technology Brief about distance education intended to influence the development and application of new and emerging technologies (NEA, 1999). "In the rush to utilize new technology to increase learning opportunities," the brief states, "educational quality must be maintained" (p. 1). The brief goes on to list and discuss a number of standards expected for courses taught at a distance, many of which are shown in Table 5.1. Like the Netcourse Evaluation Board standards, the NEA standards include both instructional standards and operational standards, as can be seen in the table.

VHS later commissioned a second panel to develop standards. This was the expert panel, convened by SRI, which developed standards in the areas of curriculum/content, pedagogy, course design, and assessment (shown in Figure 3.2). The standards are sufficiently general that they can be applied to any high school netcourse, and the panel used them to review a dozen sample Net-Courses. For example, standard 11 states that "The course integrates multiple methods of instruction," where examples of methods include assigned reading, discussions, simulation, laboratories, assigned writing, critiques, peer review, and presentations. This standard is intended to apply to netcourses in any subject; indeed, it is an important goal statement that could apply to any high school course, whether or not presented via the Internet. The standards shown in Figure 3.2 are also meant to be consistent with national standards. Standard 1, for example, refers to learning "important information, skills, and major ideas from multiple viewpoints," where the details are specific to a discipline. VHS now provides links to a wide variety of national and state standards on its Web site, and instructors in the TLC work with teachers to be sure that new courses reflect national standards. For most courses, the VHS catalog provides information about how those courses meet national standards.

Standards for Postsecondary Netcourses. Detailed standards for netcourses at the high school level, such as those in Table 5.1 and Figure 3.2, are relatively new. However, as Internet-based courses proliferated at the postsecondary level—where hundreds of degree programs can now be taken online—a

Table 5.1

Excerpt from NEA Technology Brief on Distance Education

The National Education Association believes that quality distance education can create or extend learning opportunities not otherwise available to all students.

The Association also believes that, to ensure quality, distance education courses must—

a. Be at least as rigorous as similar courses delivered by more traditional means
b. Meet accreditation standards
c. Have content that is relevant, accurate, meets state and local standards, and is subject to the normal processes of collegial decision making
d. Meet the objectives and requirements outlined in the official course description
e. Have student/faculty ratios that ensure the active engagement of students and high academic achievement
f. Have appropriate procedures mutually agreed upon by the instructor and the institution for evaluation and verification that the student is submitting his/her own work
g. Have instructors whose qualifications are the same as those of instructors teaching in traditional classes and who are prepared specifically and comprehensively to teach in this environment
h. Be integrated into the mission and consistent with the overall offerings of the institution
i. Provide fair use exemptions for participants' access to copyrighted materials for educational purposes.

The Association further believes that the institution offering the course must provide—

a. Adequate infrastructure
b. Appropriate facilities and equipment
c. Libraries and laboratories as needed
d. Adequate support and technical personnel on or off campus.

number of organizations became concerned years earlier about establishing standards to help assure quality for the courses and the programs. As early as 1996, the Western Cooperative for Educational Telecommunications (part of the Western Interstate Commission for Higher Education, or WICHE) published *Principles of Good Practice for Electronically Offered Academic Degree and Certificate Programs.* More recently, the Southern Regional Education Board published *Principles of Good Practice: The Foundation for Quality of the Electronic Campus of the Southern Regional Education Board* (Southern Regional Education Board, 2000). The purpose of this publication is to "help students find and enroll in high-quality courses and programs at colleges and universities in SREB states" and to assist institutions, for example, by guiding "the development of electronically delivered programs and courses to ensure that characteristics of good teaching and learning are addressed."

Similarly, early in 2001, the American Federation of Teachers (AFT) released a report and a set of quality standards for college-based distance education courses and programs. This report included a number of cautions. For example, the report warned that "educational quality, not financial gain, should guide where, when and how distance education is employed." The president of the AFT, Sandra Feldman, was quoted as saying, "While online and distance learning are in general good options for taking a particular course or a set of courses, this does not automatically mean that it is acceptable for an entire undergraduate degree program to have no in-class component" (American Federation of Teachers, 2001). The AFT report also focuses on protection of intellectual property rights and proper training for college faculty and on other issues designed to protect participants and help assure high quality.

The AFT guidelines and other sets of standards at the higher education level (e.g., Institute for Higher Education Policy, 2000) cover a wide range of other topics as well. There are standards for curriculum and instruction (e.g., "qualified faculty provide appropriate supervision of the program or course that is offered electronically"), for institutional context and commitment (e.g., "the program or course is consistent with the institution's role and mission" and "enrolled students have reasonable and adequate access to student services and resources appropriate to support their learning"), and for evaluation and assessment (e.g., "the institution evaluates program and course effectiveness, including assessments of student learning, student retention, and student and faculty satisfaction"). The issues raised by Internet-based courses and programs are varied and complex.

Conclusions. There are a number of lessons to be drawn about standards as they relate to online courses. We have learned that VHS has a commitment to establishing and using standards for netcourses. VHS developed and uses criteria and standards for its own purposes, especially in the TLC and the NIM.

In addition, VHS has contributed to the discussion of standards in the wider education community. We have learned that higher education institutions have begun to use standards across institutions and regions as one way of helping both developers and consumers of electronic courses and programs, and that the NEA is promoting such standards at the secondary school level. As more people become interested in high school netcourses, the need for widely accepted, easily understood sets of standards will grow.

Technology and Educational Change

As was pointed out in Chapter 1, the rhetoric surrounding the introduction of new technologies often borders on the utopian. Some promoters of virtual schools are no different from their predecessors who touted earlier technologies, setting forth grandiose claims of what virtual schooling may be able to accomplish. Even the limited experience to date with actual online schools suggests that the rhetoric needs to be tempered.

Costs. The claim that online schools can reduce costs and increase the efficiency of instruction (an example of which was cited in Chapter 1) must be moderated. VHS did allow schools to offer courses that they could not offer otherwise and thus appeal to a larger student population than was in their immediate area, and this result is significant. But the claim that this could be done without additional cost did not bear out. The participation fees, the costs of training teachers and coordinators, and the release time for coordinators are all additional costs and are substantial. Administrators and teachers both reported that the costs of VHS in time and money were greater than expected. Nonetheless, they felt that these costs were justified and the program was worthy of continuation.

Pedagogy. The claim that online schooling can support pedagogical change must also be moderated. VHS teachers reported that they did employ constructivist strategies, but no more than they did in their regular courses. Other researchers (Means & Olson, 1995) have reviewed a number of classrooms in which there is a strong relationship between technology use and pedagogical reform. They found that such pedagogical changes were supported by a number of other changes within the school as well, such as increased technical support, strong school leadership and a vision for the use of technology in classrooms, and increased time for teacher planning. VHS was not designed to foster whole-school reform of this sort. Rather, it was designed to enable schools, teachers, and students to participate in courses that would not be available otherwise. This it did. That teachers were able to use some of the constructivist pedagogical strategies that they also used in their regular courses is so much the better.

However, for the most part, current online educational environments are tightly designed around the standard educational grammar. Although a few virtual schools, such as Intelligent Education, Inc. (IEI), are cautiously moving away from the standard model toward a less teacher-oriented educational model, VHS and other schools have all the trappings of bricks-and-mortar schools: teachers, courses, credit hours, schedules, and assignments. These similarities in design make it easier for schools and teachers to adopt this new approach to distance learning and fit it into their current structure. Also, many of these features are necessitated by the fact that the movement is still novel and not yet given full credibility by the educational establishment. So the more they look like "real schools," the more credibility they can muster. But at the same time, the similarities also minimize the innovativeness of virtual programs and their ability to contribute to educational reform and change.

The Role of Teachers. Perhaps the most significant change that is enabled by VHS's approach to online schooling is the increased professionalism and authority of the participating teachers. In the VHS model, the teachers have considerable authority to create new courses and design educational materials and activities, while still addressing the demands for high quality. They are able to collaborate with an extended community of colleagues and experts who help to support their efforts and assure the quality of their courses. And they are able to offer their new courses to a population of students across the country. All of this is enabled by the technological tools provided by the VHS program. It is in sharp contrast to the typical in-school experience of most teachers, who teach ready-made courses using standard textbooks. It also contrasts with other online models in which teachers play only an incidental role of online coach or mentor or teacher of a course developed by someone else.

Indeed, it seems that the central role of the online teacher is not only a hallmark of the VHS model but is a significant reason for its success. VHS teachers are provided with training, collaborative support, tools, and a well-crafted model of online schooling. This model taps the passion and commitment of teachers and empowers them to create positive, effective learning experiences for their students. This is certainly a valuable educational change supported by technology and the VHS model.

Learning More About Virtual Schools

The rapid evolution of virtual schools means that large numbers of parents, school board members, and others with a stake in this new phenomenon are probably unaware that such options even exist for high school students. Accrediting agencies, state boards of education, local school boards, potential students in virtual high schools, their parents, and many others need to make informed decisions about this new form of schooling. Articles in the popular press can and do help to provide valuable information about virtual schools. Nonetheless, journalism cannot be a substitute for more intensive efforts to collect and analyze data about virtual high schools. Data from research—such as reported in this book or in the FVS evaluation (Bigbie & McCarroll, 2000), from virtual schools' self-evaluations, from state-sponsored studies or investigations, or from other reliable sources—will continue to be an important source of knowledge to help people make better decisions about virtual high schools. State and federal agencies are likely to play especially important roles in making more and better information available, acting both as funding sources for research, and (especially for the states) as branches of government that can require virtual schools to gather certain data and then make it available, either to the public or to the appropriate agencies.

Conclusions

VHS and other virtual high schools have rapidly proven themselves more successful than most people would have predicted 5 years ago. By the last year of the federal grant, for example, VHS was exceeding its own goals for the number of participating schools, serving about 200 high schools during the 2000–2001 academic year. The sheer number of virtual schools now operating is also an indicator of the success of the idea of providing credit-bearing netcourses to high school students.

Although a variety of viable models of virtual schooling have developed, the consortium model used by VHS has proven to have many strengths, including enlisting the talents of excellent teachers in hundreds of schools. Creating a successful "collaboration model" was one of VHS's original goals, and it has achieved this goal. The fact that the consortium approach fits easily into the existing school grammar is another important reason for its success.

The Teachers Learning Conference was an important part of the original vision of VHS. Implementing the TLC effectively was a prominent goal for VHS, and both the TLC and the NIM have proven to be significant contributors to VHS's success.

From the outset, the use of site coordinators was another important part of the VHS model. This component of VHS, too, has proven both important and successful. Each year, more virtual schools are implementing similar approaches, such as using local mentors to help online students. However, the added expense of supporting the coordinators remains an important contributor to the costs of virtual schooling.

LearningSpace, the course delivery technology used by VHS, has proven to have both important strengths and significant weaknesses. The familiar LearningSpace metaphors, such as the CourseRoom, work well for courses of vastly different types, and students are able to adapt to the technology relatively quickly, but the version of LearningSpace used by VHS has limited capabilities that prevent synchronous communication and also makes certain other types of communication difficult.

VHS and other virtual schools report relatively high dropout and stopout rates for students. At least for the present, online courses demand greater independence and responsibility of students than face-to-face courses do. As a result, enrolling in a virtual school is a decision that the students, their parents, guidance counselors, and others need to consider carefully.

With fewer social and emotional supports available online, course quality becomes even more important in netcourses than in face-to-face courses. A wide variety of steps need to be taken to help assure course quality, ranging from careful selection of teachers and effective training to monitoring of courses while they are delivered to be sure that they meet high standards. Virtual schools therefore need a thoughtful, effective administrative team. VHS's team has earned high marks overall from participants.

Written standards for offering and supporting effective online courses are available from a number of sources and are intended to help both course providers and "consumers." Online course developers, teachers, school administrators, parents, and students will benefit from understanding these standards.

Finally, the history of VHS and other virtual schools helps to illuminate both the benefits and the difficulties of using technology to achieve "education reform." Netcourses do overcome certain barriers of place and time, allowing students to take courses that otherwise would not be available. At the same time, the promises made for online technologies as a way of improving curriculum or instruction have yet to be delivered.

Nonetheless, VHS is an excellent example of Tyack and Cuban's (1995) hybridizing model of educational reform. Under this model, programs of reform are treated as hypotheses, and teachers are encouraged to create hybrids that are suited to their specific contexts and needs. In the VHS model, teachers are provided with training, collaborative support, and tools that enable them to create their own syllabus, course materials, and activities, and to offer courses to students all over the country who would not have access to them otherwise. As Tyack and Cuban point out, this kind of "tinkering" may have a far greater prospect for successful school reform than mandates imposed from above or outside the school system.

Chapter 6

THE FUTURE OF VIRTUAL HIGH SCHOOLS

The Internet and the World Wide Web have rapidly become pervasive in the lives of tens of millions of Americans. Thirty-seven percent of full-time workers have access to the Internet at work, and of those, 72% believe that it has improved their ability to do their jobs (Szuhaj & Ledger, 2001). More than 55 million Americans use the Internet daily for any number of activities, including to shop, to get news, to find information, to pay taxes, and to communicate with family, friends, or co-workers. In this environment, the emergence of new providers of virtual secondary education, including many that have been described in earlier chapters and others that have not, should not be a shock. But will the fledgling virtual schools have staying power and real impact, or will they go the way of the dot-com boom, which raised investors' expectations far beyond what was reasonable before the boom suddenly became a bust? In this chapter, we venture beyond the available data and look ahead to what the future may bring for virtual secondary schooling.

There are many fascinating surprises in the story of virtual secondary education. In the past, elementary and secondary education have not attracted many business entrepreneurs, yet now suddenly a number of prominent investors and firms find virtual schools to be an attractive investment niche. In the past, there has been much criticism of technology as a "dehumanizing influence," yet a study of 9 million women who had recently gone online for the first time found that 72% believed that e-mail enhanced their relationships with family and friends (Szuhaj & Ledger, 2001); similarly, in spite of current technology limitations, many virtual teachers and students find that communicating over the Internet is quite satisfying. Institutions of higher education have been criticized for years as places that have failed to change sufficiently with the times, continuing to use a model of education that is a thousand years old. Yet today, hundreds of degree programs and many thousands of courses are available online, setting a precedent that secondary schools will find impossible to ignore. Even the United States Army has opened an "online university," and officials predict that within 5 years as many as 80,000 soldiers may be enrolled each year (Trotter, 2001a). What new surprises does virtual secondary education hold? Can virtual schools grow to have enrollments far larger than any regular high school, for example? Will traditional schools come to view online schools as unwanted or unfair competition? Will technology radically alter the definition of schooling and the roles of teachers and students?

There is now sufficient experience in this field that trends are beginning to emerge. In this chapter, we first examine the reasons why virtual secondary education is proving appealing to many people. Then we examine potential barriers to the expansion of virtual education, including the fact that only about one-third of parents with children in school seem to approve of online learning. Next, we reexamine some of the different models of virtual secondary education, including state-based virtual high schools. Finally, we speculate about the future of VHS itself and of other virtual high schools and consider principles that may help in thinking about the future of online schools.

Why Virtual Secondary Education Is Growing

There are no reliable statistics to describe the total number of students currently enrolled in online courses throughout the United States. We do know something about the enrollments in VHS, the Florida Virtual School (FVS), and some of the other better-known virtual schools, and we do know that there are dozens of local virtual schools. Not counting any enrollments of high school students in online college courses, it appears from published figures that about 25,000 to 50,000 students were enrolled in high school netcourses during the 2000–2001 school year, or far fewer than 1% of all secondary students. That number has increased rapidly from zero in just a few years, and it seems likely to continue growing for years to come.

Four factors are particularly important in stimulating a further increase in enrollments: the proliferation of technology in schools and in society generally; the increasing legislative and political requirements that all students receive a high-quality education, regardless of where the education comes from; parental and political demands for a greater variety of educational options for children; and concerns about teacher shortages. We discuss each of these factors in turn.

Growth of Technology in Schools and Homes

Schools are spending on the order of $7 billion on technology each year, and 98% of schools in the United States are now online. The installed base of high-speed, multimedia computers in schools is now in the millions. Each year, for the same price, schools are able to obtain more powerful computer-based technologies than the year before. The growing ubiquity of technology creates a "push" that leads school administrators, parents, and business leaders to wonder what is being done to make good use of the technology available in schools.

Virtual schooling is emerging as one answer to this question. Although the reasoning may appear backwards (why not start with needs, not technology?), technology push is fueled by the American public's underlying belief that computers and other technologies are valuable tools for education.

A September 2000 survey, for example, found that 82% of the American public believe schools should invest more in technology (NASBE Study Group, 2001). This belief in the importance of technology has led states and national groups to develop educational technology standards for teachers, students, and administrators. For example, several sets of standards have been developed by the International Society for Technology in Education (2000). Colleges and universities that prepare teachers, and the institutions that provide professional development for teachers already in the schools, are aware that the public wants teachers to be able to use computers and other educational technologies effectively. As a result, a much higher proportion of younger teachers than older teachers report that teacher education programs have helped prepare them to use technology. In spite of large costs and the objections of critics who believe that schools' technology investments are misguided, there has been little public disaffection with educational technology. As new technologies continue to grow more powerful and access to the Internet becomes cheaper, easier, and ever more widespread, the public's positive opinion about the value of using technology in schools seems likely to remain very strong.

High Standards for All

Virtual schooling is also appealing to increasing numbers of educators as a way to provide equitable access to a high-quality education in America's schools. Throughout the 1980s and 1990s, there was increasing political pressure to raise student achievement for all students, including those traditionally underserved by schools. Although the ideal in the United States is to provide equal opportunity to all, the fact remains that students enroll in schools that vary greatly in quality, based on such factors as the wealth of the neighborhood in which the school is located, the demographics of the students in the school, the school's state or region, and other variables. In this climate, with its increasing emphasis on having all students meet challenging academic standards, regardless of where they live or what type of school they attend, the attraction of expanding course offerings by allowing students to learn online becomes clearer. More than 40% of high schools do not offer advanced placement (AP) courses, for example, so people are looking for other ways to provide such courses to more students. In response, the University of California started a college prep initiative (UCCP) for high school students in 1999, through its Santa Cruz campus. In the fall of 2000, according to UCCP's figures, nearly 60% of its 2,300 enrollments were through online AP courses (UCCP Program, 2001). In other states, such as Alabama, more emphasis is being given to assuring more uniform quality of the key core courses (not AP courses) for all students, even in isolated rural areas. In either case, given the growing demand for raising standards and providing students access to a wide variety of courses that cannot always be delivered locally, the continued growth of virtual schooling seems a near certainty.

The Demand for Choice

Virtual schooling also appeals to the growing numbers of parents and policy makers who seek to expand choices for American education. The growing insistence on a high-quality education for all students is just one factor that underlies a large increase in the demand by parents for alternative educational options in addition to their local public schools. Religious convictions, concerns about students' safety in school, and unhappiness with unresponsive bureaucracies are other factors leading parents to seek new options for schooling. In different localities, these options include an increase in choices permitted within the regular public schools, new charter schools (public schools that are allowed extra latitude in how they operate), or, in a few places, school vouchers for funds that families can apply toward education in a wide array of public and private schools. In addition, a growing number of parents are home-schooling their children. The growth of online schooling for high school students can be viewed as the creation of yet one more available option in a society that increasingly expects a large number of options to be available for schooling children.

Providing competition to existing public schools is one important reason why politicians and the public support more options for schooling. As the director of the Kentucky Virtual High School, Linda Pittenger, said:

> Virtual high schools are not only delivery systems for online learning, they can also function as policy levers [and] as a competitive force within the public education system by introducing new choices. (quoted in Winograd, 2002)

In the 1999–2000 school year, there were about 1,700 charter schools in the United States, up from just 2 such schools 7 years before that (Anderson et al., 2000), and that number is still increasing. The U.S. Department of Education alone is now spending more than $180 million annually to support start-up costs for new charter schools and to promote the exchange of information about how they are working (U.S. Department of Education, 2001). Former president Bill Clinton repeatedly challenged educators to create 3,000 public charter schools by the year 2002.

Some of the charter schools are online schools. These include, for example, the Pennsylvania Virtual Charter School, the Western Pennsylvania Cyber Charter School, and T.E.A.C.H.—The Einstein Academy Charter School. The state of Pennsylvania is particularly richly endowed with virtual charter schools because the state's 1997 charter-school law required that districts pay these schools the state per-pupil allocation to the district for any students from within that district who are enrolled in a virtual charter school. According to one estimate, in the fall of 2001 approximately 4,000 Pennsylvania students were enrolled in 7 so-called cyber (i.e., virtual) charter schools (KPMG Consulting, 2001).

The online charter schools appeal particularly to students who are being home-schooled. In Pennsylvania, for example, about 56% of the online charter students were previously home-schooled. However, parents who home-school their children are not the only audience. Nor are the online charters the only online schools that serve home-schooled students; as we have seen, for example, more than 40% of the FVS students are home-schooled.

The number of students schooled at home is large and growing. A recent U.S. Department of Education study estimates that about 850,000 children in the United States were schooled at home in 1999 (Gewertz, 2001). Although data for earlier years are not as reliable as many other education statistics, most people believe that the number of students being home-schooled has grown substantially in recent years, probably more than doubling between 1994 and 1999. By the time that students are of high school age, it is often increasingly difficult for their parents to provide them with the specialized knowledge or courses that they need. Online schooling therefore fills a real need in this community. A virtual school "allows my kids to take classes I don't necessarily want to teach or can't teach," says a home-schooling parent who chairs the Florida Parent-Educators Association (Trotter, 2001b). The for-profit online education venture K12, started by former secretary of education William Bennett and others, is an example of a company that is especially targeting families that are home-schooling their children. So, too, are other online schools, although not all of them. VHS, for one, has made little effort to attract home-schooled students, preferring to target students in regular public high schools as its main audience.

Home-schooled students are more likely than students enrolled in regular public schools to take multiple online courses at the same time. In Pennsylvania, for example, the 1997 law requires that virtual charter schools enroll students full time. Taking multiple courses online may be difficult for many young people, even with parental assistance—although for students who are used to being independent learners, it seems to be feasible. In Pennsylvania, online charter schools provide a live teacher to students; how often the teacher and student communicate varies. In any event, there is skepticism about the efficacy of online education for home-schoolers, and perhaps especially for elementary school students, who are a major target for K12 (but not for Apex, FVS, or many other online schools). Sandra Feldman, president of the American Federation of Teachers, speaking about the then-new K12 operation, said:

> An excellent elementary and secondary education cannot be based solely on technology. We will have to wait and see if the quality of this particular product is as grandiose as Mr. Bennett's quotes. ("Former ED Sec. Bennett," 2001)

Interestingly, even though the number of students schooled at home seems large and is growing, some industry analysts don't believe that this market niche is sufficiently large to support a business venture of significant size. Indeed, even large, for-profit online schools are typically interested in attracting a diversified clientele, including students who are home-schooled, who are enrolled in charter schools, and who are in the regular public schools.

Teacher Shortages

Another reason for school administrators' growing interest in online high schools is concern about shortages of qualified high school teachers, particularly teachers in certain specialties, such as mathematics, science, and technology. Estimates of the number of teachers needed over the next decade run over 2 million (Hussar, 1999), and it may be difficult to meet this demand through traditional means. It is true that virtual schools can make selected courses and teachers available to students who are widely distributed. In this sense, they can certainly even out the distribution of teachers and courses, which is usually "lumpy," meaning that some schools have more qualified teachers available than they need, while others have too few.

Yet the introduction of netcourses taught by real teachers does not magically multiply the number of good teachers. Thus, the idea that the Internet will give "all students" access to "the best teachers" seems naive, if the intent is to allow students a chance to actually interact with those teachers. "The best" teachers, after all, have limited time and therefore can serve only a limited number of students.

A more reasonable argument, which is made by some online schools, is that netcourses can be taught part time by teachers who otherwise would retire or stay home to care for family members. One official of an online school uses the term *home-teaching* as a play on the term *home-schooling*. In this view, online schools will help alleviate teacher shortages by allowing teachers with young children, or partially retired teachers, to teach students online. If teacher shortages are as significant as some report they will be, even part-time online assistance from qualified teachers will be viewed as an important source of help, further fueling online schooling. However, notwithstanding utopian rhetoric, there is no reason to believe that virtual high schools by themselves can make a major contribution to solving the problem of teacher shortages.

Potential Barriers to the Growth of Virtual Schooling

For the same reasons that online schooling has grown so popular recently, it seems destined to grow further in the early part of the 21st century. Yet there are also potential barriers to growth that may turn out to be serious. These include concerns about costs and quality control, skepticism about online learning among a significant number of parents of school-age children, and the possibility that the education system may reject virtual schools as too threatening.

Cost Issues

KPMG's study of Pennsylvania's cyber charter schools found that per-student costs ranged from about $5,000 to $7,000, depending on the level of services provided. This figure is comparable to the per-pupil expenditures in regular public schools, which was $6,500 in 1998–1999, according to the National Center for Education Statistics (2001). Figures cited in earlier chapters show similar per-student-semester costs for other virtual schools. However, virtual schools typically do not provide many services or facilities provided by regular schools, such as health and guidance services, laboratories, gymnasia, and theaters. Furthermore, for students who are taking only one or two online courses while enrolled in regular public schools, virtual schooling represents an added cost, not a substitute or trade-off. It is fair to say that the costs of online schools are still high—partly when compared directly with public schools' costs, but especially when viewed as an add-on to the cost of traditional courses. Therefore, it is an open question whether costs will turn out to be a significant barrier to the growth of virtual schools.

In business terms, there are many unanswered questions about the viability of virtual schooling. The required investments are large, but the returns are still uncertain. A vice president of Apex reported that it takes $100,000 to $200,000, 15 people, and nearly 8 months to develop an online AP course (NASBE Study Group, 2001, p. 42). (VHS, which depends on individual teachers to develop most of its courses, obviously spends far less on development.) Looking at all the factors that may affect business success, KPMG's study in Pennsylvania concluded that "not all new cyber schools have long-term viability" (KPMG Consulting, 2001, p. 5).

A related problem area for elementary and secondary netcourses is that the growth of technology is rarely driven by the needs of schools or young people. The free market is much more responsive to the needs of corporate training, adult and higher education, entertainment, and other sectors—because these markets are larger and promise far greater profits. One recent estimate of the size of the higher education "e-learning" market suggests that it will soon reach $2 billion annually (Flisi, 2001). The market for virtual secondary education is clearly far smaller, and, historically, elementary and secondary education have not been major factors in the development of technology. Thus, the development of good technological support systems for high school netcourses is a far lower priority for businesses than support systems for other portions of the education, training, and entertainment market. The development of LearningSpace, or any other type of software system for online schools, is expensive and will be done primarily for other market areas (such as corporations, the military, or higher education), not for K–12 students.

Quality Control

Another potential barrier is that if virtual secondary education develops a reputation for low quality, its growth potential could be seriously reduced. Not only would individual families or schools be more cautious about allowing students to enroll in online courses, but the potential exists for an institutional backlash. For example, teacher unions, including the National Education Association and the American Federation of Teachers, which are now cautiously supportive of online schooling, could instead lobby vigorously against it.

The proponents of virtual schools need to take steps, as VHS has done, to establish and enforce standards of quality that allow schools, parents, students, and others to sign up with some assurance that courses are well designed, teachers are trained to teach online, expectations for students' work are comparable to those in regular courses, and there is a process in place for maintaining standards even as changes inevitably take place in specific course offerings.

These concerns are not simply theoretical. KPMG recommends, for example, that the boards of Pennsylvania's cyber charter schools, or the chartering public school districts, "should monitor the extent to which cyber charters are having regular interaction with their students to ensure their students are appropriately supported" and that students are achieving at appropriate academic levels (KPMG Consulting, 2001, p. 9). The report suggests a number of steps that should be taken to provide more information and greater accountability about online schools. Calls for information and accountability are only likely to increase as enrollments grow.

A report titled *Virtual High Schools: State of the States*, which examined a wide variety of online high schools, also noted the importance of developing internal and external structures for assessing the quality of netcourses. The report notes, "The Netcourse™ quality standards and evaluation rubrics developed by Concord VHS and SRI are outstanding. Both have embedded continuous internal needs assessment and evaluation procedures in their online courses and administrative processes with participating districts" (Clark, 2000, pp. 24–25).

Public Readiness

Online schools are a new phenomenon and are unfamiliar to most parents and students. How ready are parents to accept online learning? Will the concerns of some parents inhibit the growth of virtual schools? Publicly available data to answer these questions are sparse. However, a Phi Delta Kappa/Gallup poll released in 2001 includes some information on these topics. According to the poll, only 35% of parents with children in school approved of allowing students to earn high school credits online via the Internet without attending school. Furthermore, of those parents who approved of the practice, just under half, 49%, said they would allow their child to go through high school taking most courses online (Rose & Gallup, 2001).

At first blush, this statistic—suggesting that only about one in six parents support the practice—seems discouraging. However, further reflection provides a much more encouraging outlook for virtual schools. First, when one considers that there are perhaps 10 million families with children in high schools, 49% of 35% of this number is still more than a million families. Considering that current online schools enroll just a tiny number of students nationwide, the growth potential for the foreseeable future seems huge. Second, the question addresses earning high school credits "without attending school," which is ambiguous. The follow-up question shows that the intent was to include students, like those taking VHS courses, who still obtain many of their credits through face-to-face courses taken in regular public high schools but who do not or need not attend school for their virtual course(s). However, the way that the first question is worded might have been interpreted to mean that students would not attend school at all, as with home-schooled students. In that case, it would be remarkable if as many as 35% of parents were ready to accept this new practice. Regardless of how the question was interpreted by those who responded to the poll, the reported finding that only a minority of parents seem ready to accept online high school courses does not appear to present a significant barrier to growth for the near future, as long as the number of students involved with online learning remains small compared with the size of the K–12 student population (more than 50 million). As online learning grows in size, more parents may come to accept it.

Rejection by the Education System

The most serious challenge to the growth of virtual schooling is the possibility that some forms of online schools, or certain practices of virtual schools, will be rejected outright or be subject to serious modifications on the basis of litigation or legislation. For example, in 2001 the Pennsylvania School Boards Association brought suit to challenge the legality of the state's law that requires school districts to pay the costs of online schools for home-schooled students (Trotter, 2001c). Nearly 60 districts in the state refused to pay more than three-quarters of a million dollars in bills presented by one of the virtual charter schools. According to the association, virtual charter schools would cost districts approximately $18 million in the 2001–2002 school year. One of the association's executives is quoted as saying, "It's an unbudgeted, expensive hit," adding that districts could not reasonably have anticipated spending these funds. A court injunction allowed the cyber school to be paid, but the state legislature commissioned the KPMG study that has been cited.

Financial questions raised about the Pennsylvania cyber charter schools include whether or not there is a clear relationship between their operating costs, the amounts they charge the regular school districts, and their profits. Other concerns about the cyber charter schools have not been about money. Questions were raised about whether student enrollment figures claimed by some of the schools were accurate and whether students enrolled in the cyber schools received adequate supervision by teachers (rather than just doing independent study).

In the face of these concerns, legislation was introduced to add greater accountability and to reduce the burden on individual school districts. The state's secretary of education, Charles Zogby, requested that the state legislature consider statewide—instead of district-by-district—approval, monitoring, and oversight of cyber charter schools.

By the time this book is published, the particular situation in Pennsylvania may be resolved. Nonetheless, concerns raised in the case are likely to remain important for years to come: concerns about the accountability of virtual schools; about the costs of online schooling; and about the relationships among existing schools, the new providers of virtual education, and the purposes of American education. One organization, the independent Center on Education Policy, which advocates for public education and more effective public schools, has developed a set of purposes and principles of American education (Center on Education Policy, 2002) leading to key questions the center believes should be asked about *any* major education reform, such as "Will the reform encourage students to get along with diverse peers and promote social cohesion and cultural unity?" The prospect that a large number of students in publicly supported cyber charter schools would not have much contact with their peers in bricks-and-mortar schools could raise a question, for some people, about whether this new educational option fails to properly promote the cohesiveness of our society at the same time that the public pays the bill.

Concerns, such as these, about how well virtual schools fit with existing schools and with differing ideas about the public good will be especially significant for those companies and institutions, possibly including VHS itself, that exist outside the boundaries of the traditional public education system. Virtual high schools created by states may be far less likely than outside groups to be challenged on legal grounds, but even they must be mindful of the new issues raised about accountability, costs, and other aspects of online schooling. Notably, state legislatures are likely to have serious reservations about any virtual schools supported with public funds that appear to be unaccountable to taxpayers or to school authorities.

Large, bureaucratic systems are usually resistant to change; the K–12 education system is notorious in this regard. Especially within this context, the rapidity with which more than a dozen states have embraced virtual schooling is remarkable. In part this enthusiasm is due to the dissatisfaction that many governors and state legislatures have expressed with the capacity of the public school system to improve sufficiently rapidly, leading them to look to new technological approaches. The capacity of the education system to change further in the face of rapid technological change is a topic to which we will return in the remainder of this chapter.

Approaches to Virtual Schooling

As noted in Chapter 1, VHS set out to "create a collaboration model that would be scalable, replicable, and feasible for all schools." To what extent has VHS actually served as a model that other providers emulated? And why is it that other approaches besides the "collaboration model" are now springing up in so many states? In this section, we explore the appeal of the different approaches to virtual schooling that have appeared in recent years.

VHS as a Model

The development of the consortium or collaborative approach, whereby schools offer netcourses and enroll students in other schools' netcourses, is one way in which VHS provides a model. This model can be contrasted with many other approaches to virtual schooling, now more common than the collaborative approach, in which local schools and regular teachers have little or no role in offering netcourses. There are some other virtual schools that use the collaborative or consortium approach. One example is CyberSchool, based in the Lane City school district in Eugene, Oregon. CyberSchool's faculty is dispersed and includes teachers at many different schools, as well as some teachers who are partially retired. However, judged simply by numbers, the collaborative approach is not proving to be the online "model" adopted by the most virtual schools. Yet, as noted earlier, more and more online schools are exploring how to involve local teachers and are expanding their offerings in this way. Thus, this "model" provided by VHS has had mixed success, working very well for participating VHS schools but not spreading as quickly to other groups outside of VHS, as the founders of VHS may have expected.

But there is a second and perhaps more important way in which VHS has provided a model. Because VHS was one of the first and became one of the largest online high schools, its experiences—as described by VHS staff at meetings and in conferences, recounted in many dozens of newspaper and magazine articles, disseminated in written evaluation reports, or made available in other forms—have become well known in the community of online schools. VHS's pioneering experience has thus allowed others to observe not just one particular approach or model for providing netcourses but also to learn more broadly about the idea, the practicality, and the desirability of providing high school courses through the Web.

There is no question that VHS's success has been an important inspiration and source of ideas to many people in the field of virtual secondary education. As Robert Youngblood, administrator of the Alabama Online High School, said:

> We had two people who took [VHS's] training. Everybody needs pioneers to figure out how things are going to work. They [VHS] really jumped head over heels into the briar patch, and they came out clean and helped the rest of us see the way.

VHS has been cited in national reports and used as an example in U.S. Department of Education presentations and publications. The staff of VHS provided demonstrations to congressional employees on Capitol Hill. One of the founders of VHS, as well as some of its staff, co-authored one of the first books about facilitating online learning (Collison, Elbaum, Haavind, & Tinker, 2000).

Not all providers of virtual secondary education have been equally successful. Writing about a different online school in which his students participated, one high school teacher reported, "Their quality is poor; courses are mostly textbooks online. Courses are not 'taught' online, but rather materials are available." Another teacher wrote about an online college program with which she was familiar that "it is not interactive [and] interaction is the key to student motivation." The fact that a new venture as visible as VHS has also been successful in reaching many of its goals has influenced both the development of virtual schooling and other people's perceptions of the efficacy of online schools.

State-Based Schools as a Model

A large number of state-based virtual high schools have appeared almost overnight. At least a dozen states already have their own, including Alabama, Arkansas, Florida, Hawaii, Illinois, Kentucky, Louisiana, Michigan, New Mexico, North Dakota, Utah, and West Virginia. Virtual schooling has become a topic of keen political interest, with many of these states' governors highly visible in announcements and press conferences about the creation of virtual schools. The governor of Kentucky, for example, said that the state wants to catch up with the academic performance of other states and hopes to make the learning process "more efficient" through its online school. A Virtual High School Symposium in October 2000 brought representatives of a large number of these online schools together in the Washington, D.C., area; a keynote address was given by the associate director of the White House Office of Science and Technology Policy.

The state-based model of a virtual high school is clearly proving to be popular. Matching courses to state standards and state needs is one advantage of the state-based model, assuming this matching is done well. If the state education system itself supports an online school, problems arising about the accreditation of courses are likely to be reduced. However, as we have seen earlier, national virtual schools, such as VHS, are not encountering major problems having their courses accepted for credit, so the issue of accreditation may not be a great competitive advantage to state schools. Approval by the governor, the state board of education, or other state officials immediately lends legitimacy to the effort.

Conversely, one potential problem with state-based virtual schools involves using courses developed for one state in a state with different standards and needs. At the least, time may need to be spent correlating such courses for different standards.

Elementary and secondary education in the United States are primarily the responsibility of state governments. This fact, as much as any other, probably explains why so many state-based virtual high schools have appeared. Education officials and other political leaders in the states are eager to adopt new initiatives that they view as likely to improve schooling. As we have seen, state-based virtual schools can also work closely with national providers.

Colleges and Universities

Colleges and universities are also emerging as important providers of netcourses to high schools. In some cases, universities have created special programs for high school students. Examples include Indiana University High School, the Stanford University Education Program for Gifted Youth, the University of California College Prep initiative, and the University of Nebraska Independent Study High School.

In addition, many colleges and universities permit high school students to take courses for credit. VHS teachers responding to an item on one of the surveys conducted for the evaluation said that they know of students who are taking online courses from California State University at Fullerton, Eastern Idaho Technical College, Brigham Young University, the University of Maryland, Montana State University, and the University of Massachusetts in Boston. This is just a small sampling of colleges and universities allowing, or even encouraging, high school students to take courses online. As secondary schools continue to raise standards for students, the market for offering and awarding college credits to high school students (and charging associated fees) is likely to grow at least as fast as the predicted overall growth of online learning at the postsecondary level.

Consumer Preferences

The collaborative model of virtual schools, the state-based virtual schools, and netcourses provided by colleges and universities are some of the "models" of online schooling now serving high school students. National for-profit providers, virtual charter schools, and district- or school-based virtual schools (such as HISD Virtual School in Houston, Texas, and CyberSchool in Juneau, Alaska) are other "models" also serving high school students.

There appears to be room for many different approaches to virtual schooling, and each has certain advantages. For example, state-based virtual schools can more easily be guaranteed to meet state standards, and these schools typically obtain state funding, which may help them to assure a stable base to build on. On the other hand, national schools can aggregate demand for thin courses even more than state schools, and the national model appears to be more attractive to business entrepreneurs. School- and district-based approaches allow the greatest degree of local participation and control over online course content. It is too soon to know which models the majority of people will prefer.

Private business interests have undoubtedly commissioned surveys to examine parental preferences, but such information is not likely to be publicly available. There are, however, some data from the VHS evaluation concerning opinions about the variety of providers of high school netcourses. Nearly half of the VHS principals, and about one-third of the VHS site coordinators and teachers, were familiar with other programs offering virtual courses. Asked about the other program they knew best, many respondents reported that those programs offered courses of high quality (according to 60% of principals and coordinators, and 50% of teachers). Asked whether the program they knew best had a site coordinator (as VHS does), fewer than one-third of teachers and coordinators said yes.

The principals were asked whether they preferred a national program or a program serving only their state. Only 6% preferred a program serving just their state, but 38% said both types were equally attractive. Another 37% felt a national program would be more attractive, and 19% were unsure. To some extent, this is a biased sample because the VHS participants chose to participate in a national program in the first place. Even so, it does not appear that this group of "consumers" has an overwhelming preference for one type of program over another. In other words, for those, like VHS's participants, who already understand what virtual schooling is all about, course quality, cost, accreditation, and other factors may be more important issues in selecting a provider than whether the approach used to deliver the online courses is national, state, or local in scope, or whether the approach is collaborative or centralized.

What Does the Future Hold?

All the virtual high schools are relatively young and are still learning what they need to do to serve their clientele and how to do it well. For example, FVS's administrators discovered, to their surprise, that in Florida the most popular courses are the ones students can get at their local schools, like American Government. By taking such a course online, students are able to free up a slot to take another, different, face-to-face course, and this capability turns out to be important for many students. VHS, of course, operates with a very different assumption, namely, that schools want to offer students many courses that otherwise could not be provided to them. Given the uncertainties that the schools face, and the surprises that they encounter as they put new ideas into action, it is hardly surprising that the number, types, and offerings of the virtual schools are still evolving. For virtual schooling, continuing growth and a rapidly changing landscape are the two near certainties for the foreseeable future.

The Future of VHS

In the fall of 2001, VHS crossed an important threshold, moving from its organizational links with Hudson Public Schools and the Concord Consortium to a new status as an independent, not-for-profit organization: VHS, Inc. VHS has moved from fiscal dependence on the federal Challenge Grant to become a self-supporting organization that charges schools for services. Liz Pape, the CEO, and other staff believe that VHS, Inc. has a bright future and will make the transition to independent status successfully. The fact that a majority of participating schools have continued to participate in VHS and pay the required fees provides an important basis for this optimism.

Although VHS was a bold experiment, the key participants say they knew from an early date that virtual high schools would take off and become successful. They do express some disappointment that so many state-based virtual schools have been created and have offered a wide variety of courses (their own, or others'), but not made space in their catalogs for VHS's course offerings. In many cases, the state-based schools came to VHS staff for advice about how to set up a virtual school. In the views of key VHS staff, the primary reason that so many state-based schools have been created is that doing so saves state and local educators the effort of aligning unfamiliar courses, such as those VHS offers, with the state standards. Despite the fact that information is provided about most VHS courses that shows their alignment with national standards, states and localities still need to tie the courses to state or local standards.

VHS's strategies for providing online schooling have evolved. The original emphasis on one-of-a-kind courses is now supplemented by offering multiple sections of popular courses. To support this evolution, the Teachers Learning Conference (TLC) for teachers who will design their own course is now supplemented by the NetCourse Instructional Methodologies (NIM) for teachers who want to learn to teach a section of a course designed by someone else. A great many revisions and improvements have been made regarding school policies and procedures, how students sign up for courses, how and when grades are reported, and other important topics.

Yet much about VHS's philosophy has remained the same. The reliance on scheduled asynchronous learning means that there is little enthusiasm for adding "chat" or other features that require participants to be online at the same time. VHS's emphasis on interactions between and among the teacher and students in each course remains as strong as ever and is one of the central themes in the professional development offered teachers through the TLC and NIM courses. VHS's interest in making online learning a supplement to students' participation in regular schools is still a central part of its philosophy. VHS staff believe that online learning should never be a replacement for the normal social interactions of adolescents, academic and otherwise, and they still have much more interest in serving regular schools than families who home-school their children. Students participating in VHS still spend most of their academic time in regular classrooms, not online.

However, evolution will continue. VHS continues to refine its application process for teachers, making it more difficult to be accepted. Applicants must submit essays online, and all applications are carefully reviewed. The teacher professional development courses continue to be refined and improved. Like a number of other virtual high schools, VHS expects an increasing number of its teachers to be retirees, who no longer work in regular schools, or teachers who have temporarily stopped full-time teaching.

The Future of Other Virtual Schools

Discussions with leaders of more than half a dozen virtual schools uncovered a number of common themes in their views of the future. Aside from the near-universal view that virtual schooling will continue to grow, perhaps the most important among the views expressed is a belief that online learning's greatest potential lies in integration with regular schools. Clearly, the entrepreneurs who are targeting home-schoolers will have a somewhat different point of view, and even those for whom home-schooled students are a minority, such as FVS, will pay attention to the home-schooling community and its demand for netcourses. However, for most providers of virtual schooling, both the growing size of the market for netcourses and many of the interesting business and education issues are tied to the relationship between online learning and regular schools.

On the one hand, the virtual schools are already witnessing a rapid acceptance by many states, districts, and administrators of the idea of online learning. Many psychological barriers are disappearing, at least among key policy makers, such as governors, chief state school officers, and district superintendents. Virtual schooling is becoming part of the mainstream.

At the same time, leaders of virtual schools believe that online learning is now and will continue to be a challenge to many "sacred cows" in education. Where are students and teachers required to be when they participate in courses, and when is that participation permitted to happen? Is "seat time" important? Changing many key parts of the familiar school grammar may come as a shock to many people. Yet one commissioner of education in a state that supports a virtual school noted that his state's leadership is ready to challenge important traditions in education, such as the idea that course credit be based only on Carnegie units or that state funding to schools be tied to students' physical daily attendance.

The prospect of rapid change is both exciting and anxiety-provoking. One virtual school administrator said, "It scares us what could change," and described the possibility that a district superintendent might decide that instead of hiring a teacher to move from high school to high school to teach a subject with relatively low demand, the decision might be to hire that same teacher to teach online, simultaneously serving students in multiple schools. As long as the teacher in this scenario was a regular district employee, few hackles might be raised. But suppose more and more teachers become independent contractors, as many of the virtual school administrators expect? Some resistance to changing the status of teachers is likely to arise, and, as in the Pennsylvania charter-school litigation, both the public school system and the virtual schools may be forced to respond.

Another common theme identified by the leaders was their perception that schools and districts are eager to get access to netcourses from a variety of sources. As a result, many virtual schools package or bundle courses that have been created by different institutions under different auspices. The leaders' perception of what "the market" wants mirrors the findings of the VHS survey, cited above, indicating that a variety of netcourse providers seem acceptable to administrators. In some cases, according to the leaders interviewed, schools and districts not only want a variety of offerings but also insist on being able to modify them as needed.

Many of the virtual schools continue to be concerned about issues that are by now familiar to the reader. For example, one leader said that assuring quality instruction online is "what keeps me awake at night." Leaders are concerned about training teachers to support interaction and a high level of engagement by students, and they are concerned about putting the right kinds of support structures in place at participating schools. These are issues that VHS has focused on for years.

Making good use of technology for virtual schools is also on the leaders' minds. Some of the schools use 800 phone numbers (free to callers), and some require that teachers speak with their students on a regular basis. A number of virtual schools are using synchronous chat capabilities—for example, as a way for teachers to have "office hours." Others are experimenting with shared online whiteboards and with desktop video that allows people to see live moving pictures of one another through the Internet. All the leaders are aware of how rapidly technology is changing and of the importance of continuing to adapt their uses of technology to support students and teachers—as are other experts in technology and education, who suggest that the increasing power of computer and telecommunications technologies will have dramatic influences on virtual schooling.

The Future Development of Technology

Jeremy Roschelle and Roy Pea, researchers at SRI International's Center for Technology in Learning, wrote an article in 1999 that described some of the limitations of today's Internet and discussed prospects for the future (Roschelle & Pea, 1999). Although they realize that decisions about current uses of technology need to be made now, Roschelle and Pea argue that it is premature to judge the long-term value of Internet technologies for learning. They wrote:

> Although the web may be attractive for some K–12 and educational research projects now, we believe that there are major weaknesses which must be addressed by further innovation before the Internet becomes a key tool for learning communities. Moreover, the Internet five years from now is likely to be more different from today's Internet than today's Internet is from prior bulletin board and conferencing systems. (1999, p. 25)

As an example, Roschelle and Pea argued that the Internet has to become a medium that can take much better advantage of visualization, simulation, and modeling capabilities than is typically the case in online courses. Science and mathematics courses, for example, would benefit from highly engaging and interactive simulations online, but courses in most virtual schools do not make use of such capabilities; most netcourses have no such capabilities at all. Another concern is that today's interactive communication on the Web is primarily dependent on text—a concern that is clearly applicable to VHS and other virtual high schools. Not only does text pose a barrier to students with poor reading and writing skills, it also takes much longer to use a keyboard to enter text than it does to speak, which is one reason why teaching a netcourse is so time-consuming. Advances in computer technologies and the Internet over the next 10 to 20 years will change this situation dramatically, allowing live voice and video to become cheap and ubiquitous on the Web.

Futurist and noted technology inventor Ray Kurzweil (1999) predicts that by the year 2009 computers in a wide variety of shapes, sizes, and functions will pervade our lives. He predicts that people will commonly have up to a dozen computers on and around their bodies, embedded in clothing, jewelry, and other body objects, such as eyeglasses and wristwatches. These computers will be wirelessly networked to each other and to other networks to give continuous access to integrated, digital, multimedia objects. Learning at a distance will be commonplace and will extend throughout one's lifetime. By 2019, Kurzweil goes on to predict, communication with computers will take place largely through spoken language and gestures, three-dimensional displays will be common, and computers will begin to have "automated personalities." Displays will be so good that "a person can be fooled as to whether or not another person is physically present or is being projected through electronic communication" (Kurzweil, 1999, p. 205). Clearly, technological innovations such as these will have significant impacts on the nature of virtual schooling—for example, by making netcourses more accessible to students who are not good readers, even allowing virtual education to become especially valuable to students who need extra help in their regular classes. Kurzweil further predicts that by 2019, 20 years after his book was published, most learning will be accomplished by using intelligent software-based simulated teachers, which presumably could be used as part of, or in conjunction with, online courses. Venturing even farther into the future, by 2029, he says, machines will begin to have consciousness.

Kurzweil's predictions, which are optimistic about the benefits that powerful technology will bring, return us to the utopian theme with which this book began. Yet the impact of technology on education that is evident from the perspective of VHS and other virtual high schools has a far more incremental character. Predicting the development of technology is relatively easy compared with predicting the impact that technology will have on human activity and organizations.

The Impacts of Technology and the Future of Virtual Schools

It is not necessary to challenge Kurzweil's predictions about technological developments to conclude that their impacts on virtual schools over the next 10 to

20 years are likely to be more limited. As Harvard's Chris Dede (1998) and others point out, the most significant barriers to educational innovation are not technical or even economic, but psychological, organizational, political, and cultural. The ultimate impact that technology will have on education over the next decade or two will deeply depend on how these emerging technological capabilities do or do not dovetail with, enable, and reinforce society's vision of and goals for schools. Technology will interact with trends at the micro or classroom level, such as trends in curriculum, pedagogy, and assessment, and changes in the roles of teachers and students. Simultaneously, technology will interact with other trends at the macro level, including the organization and governance of schools, as well as the ways in which parents, businesses, and community organizations are involved in the life of schools and students.

Technology at the Classroom Level. For example, at the classroom level, if certain developments continue in project-based, constructivist pedagogy (Bransford, Brown, & Cocking, 2000) and performance assessment (Pellegrino, Glaser, & Chudowsky, 2001), and if these are tied to efforts to better connect schools with workplaces, families, and communities, technological developments can make a significant synergistic contribution—not only in virtual schools but in schools more broadly. Many writers have discussed how technological advances might influence the daily lives of teachers and students when they align with these corollary developments. In the vision of education's near-future described by Kozma and Schank (1998), technology will allow both students and teachers to work more easily in teams—sometimes meeting in the same place and sometimes connected with other resources and people, such as other teachers and students, parents, scientists, and businesspeople who are geographically distributed. Team members will draw on the complementary skills and knowledge of their fellow students to design research, conduct studies, search for information, create products, and give presentations that integrate mathematics, science, and language. Many more students than at present will develop skills that allow them to work together and address or even solve complex real-world problems.

In this vision, networked resources and computer-supported collaborative environments, including those available in virtual schools, will give both students and teachers "just-in-time" access to remote libraries, museums, and laboratories, as well as to experts, parents, and community members who have specialized knowledge, who have the same concerns, or who are working on the same kinds of problems and projects that are motivating student learning. These environments, which in the future will be a common feature of virtual schools, will allow teachers, students, and others to simultaneously view and discuss the same resources and jointly use online tools to collaborate on shared projects, although these other people may be located in different places. Collaborative environments will connect teachers to their colleagues and other experts who can support their work, assist in their professional development, and provide ideas and advice as teachers respond to students' needs and ideas. Teachers and students will also have access to a variety of personal devices and constructivist tools that enable them to organize their work, search for information, conduct studies, collect and analyze data, and create and disseminate products—not just reports or PowerPoint presentations but their own simulations, multimedia productions, and Web-based resources. In the background, technologies such as dynamic, linked curriculum, assessment, and student databases will support teachers by helping them connect students' emerging interests and developing skills to demanding curricular goals and requirements, so as to both challenge student learning and document its accomplishment.

The vision described by Kozma and Schank is modest in the technological advances that it assumes. However, it is bold in envisioning the use of technology to reinforce a set of intersecting pedagogical, curricular, and cultural changes in education that take advantage of these technological developments. Whether these changes will take place is an open question. Alternatives are also possible, including the possibility that the potential benefits of technology for increasing teamwork and for learning advanced skills simply will not be well used by schools, either the bricks-and-mortar or the virtual kind.

Technology and the Organization of Schools. There are similar open questions at the macro level, that is, concerning the organization, funding, and governance of schools. The organization and governance of the education system have already been changing rapidly, with large increases in the numbers of charter schools and of home-schooled students, and with much more interest in and commitment to allowing private businesses to participate in managing schools. At the same time, technology has allowed virtual schools to begin to challenge such long-standing components of the school grammar as that teachers and students need to be in the same place at the same time or that students must log a certain number of hours of "seat time" to be awarded credit for taking a course—ideas that currently drive funding formulas as well as people's concepts of what schooling ought to be. How will these various changes intersect? What will be the impacts of virtual schools on teacher certification requirements, funding formulas, and the relationship between the public and private sectors? Will greatly increased numbers of families accept the idea that schooling need not take place in a building called a school, and, if so, what will be the impacts on current school systems? Will virtual schooling increase the speed of changes in organization and governance?

VHS: Changing Schools from the Inside. Tyack and Cuban (1995) observe that the educational system in the United States is extremely resistant to radical change. In response, they advocate a process of reform that works from the inside out, especially by enlisting the support and skills of teachers as key actors in reform. They view this approach as a positive kind of tinkering that knowledgeably adapts reform to local needs and circumstances, preserving what is valuable and correcting what is not. Under this approach, reforms are treated as hypotheses and teachers are encouraged to create hybrids suited to their context, their needs, and the needs of their students. Change is incremental—evolution, rather than revolution.

From 1996 to 2001, the staff of the Virtual High School were effective in harnessing this incremental model of change and connecting it to the new resources of the early version of the educational Web. In designing VHS, the staff gave teachers a general structure and, through the TLC and NIM, a set of skills, and then let the teachers use their own energy and the resources of the Web to create a set of courses that were valued by administrators and students. Through VHS, schools were able to offer, teachers were able to teach, and students were able to take courses that were not available to them otherwise.

This "hybridizing" model of reform allows teachers and schools to adopt technology in ways that they understand and that are consistent with current structures, pressures, and constraints. On the other hand, VHS and other virtual schools as yet have introduced few changes in pedagogy of the sort envisioned by Kozma and Schank. The online courses are much like traditional courses in bricks-and-mortar schools. Teachers spent a lot of time preparing materials, interacting with students, and grading assignments. They used the same kinds of pedagogical techniques as they do in their regular courses. Students read materials, prepared assignments, and engaged in discussions, although not as often as in their regular courses.

In VHS, teachers and students had difficulty collaborating with each other, and rarely did they interact with anyone in VHS other than the teacher and students in their immediate course. It was difficult to use multimedia effectively. Yet, as they did in their regular classes, VHS teachers reported that they engaged their online students in inquiry-based projects, related school learning to the real world, and had students create products, even though they were often written essays. Unlike the regular school experience, teachers were more likely to interact and collaborate with other teachers in VHS. And both teachers and students had and enjoyed the flexibility of being able to work when and where they wanted. There were no "seat-time" requirements.

A Larger Transformation. Perhaps the development of VHS is the first step in some larger transformation. VHS and the hybridizing model present schools and teachers with a mechanism by which they can use technology to make incremental change over time. By themselves, technological developments over the next decade or so will permit some of the deficiencies that VHS teachers and students encountered to be addressed. The visualization, simulation, and modeling capabilities cited by Roschelle and Pea will provide students with online materials that are more interactive and include more multimedia. Communication and collaboration problems will be resolved. But more dramatic innovation at the classroom level will occur only as teachers leverage these and other technological advances to bootstrap other changes in pedagogy, curriculum, and assessment. The future envisioned by Kozma and Schank will be realized if, over time, these incremental changes increase the amount of project-based work that students are engaged in, if they increase the amount of collaboration among students and between students and others in the outside world, and if students are involved in the construction of sophisticated products and presentations that address complex real-world problems and meet high standards of learning.

However, the rest of the world will not be standing still as the current education system makes incremental changes. Computer-based technology, a "disruptive" (some say revolutionary) force that has pushed many industries and social practices to change far faster than they would have otherwise, will rapidly develop further. In Michigan, a discussion is beginning about whether to require *all* high school students to take at least one virtual course. Online testing of students is already becoming more common (e.g., Virginia is developing the capability to do its end-of-course testing of high school students online), potentially making it easier and cheaper in the future to provide students with credits based on their performance rather than on "seat time." The increasing use of audio and video on the Web will make it feasible to provide Internet-based assistance to students who are not good readers and/or whose first language is not English, thereby expanding the potential market for online tutoring and test-preparation businesses to a much greater size than exists today. Artificially intelligent tutoring systems that rival human tutors in specific domains, such as algebra, may be deployed through the Internet and offered to parents, students, or school systems, at a price. Colleges and universities, which already offer thousands of virtual courses, may attract a growing number of high school students to enroll online, either in addition to or in lieu of taking certain high school courses. Amidst these potential changes, a host of questions may arise—about accountability, about the role of schools in promoting social cohesion, about equitable access to expensive services by low-income families, about the amount of time young people spend online, and about other issues.

Which particular new services will flourish online is difficult to predict. What seems certain is that commercial ventures will continue to emerge—and often fade away—as they seek out lucrative and workable models for delivering online education. Parents will select among the increasing number of options for educating their children, both within and outside of the public school system. Governors and other elected officials will continue to look for ways to increase student achievement as they define it. The challenge to the schools, as managed by the political system, will be to make changes rapidly enough in response to technological and other changes that the mass of parents and students will not "vote with their feet" and find other alternatives. The early signs are positive. Governors, chief state school officers, and other key policy makers seem determined to embrace interesting, innovative approaches that make use of powerful technology. VHS and other virtual high schools have quickly found a place within the public school system, and it seems likely that they will expand, evolve, and satisfy the needs and the preferences of growing numbers of students and teachers.

REFERENCES

Alis Technologies. (1997). Web languages hit parade. (Available at: http://alis.isoc.org/palmares.en.html)

American Federation of Teachers. (2001, January 17). *Is online education off course? New AFT report proposes standards for online colleges.* Press release. (Available at: http://www.electroniccampus.org/student/srecinfo/publications/principles.asp)

Anderson, L., Adelman, N., Yamashiro, K., Donnelly, M. B., Finnigan, K., Blackorby, J., & Cotton, L. (2000). *Evaluation of the public charter schools program: Year one evaluation report.* Washington, DC: U.S. Department of Education.

Anderson, R., & Ronnkvist, A. (1999). *The presence of computers in American schools.* Irvine, CA: Center for Research on Information Technology and Organizations.

Berman, S. H., & Pape, E. (2001, October). A consumer's guide to online courses. *The School Administrator, 58*(9), 14–18. (Available at: www.aasa.org)

Bigbie, C., & McCarroll, W. (2000). *The Florida high school evaluation 1999–2000 report.* Tallahassee: Florida State University.

Bransford, J., Brown, A., & Cocking, R. (2000). *How people learn: Brain, mind, experience, and school.* Washington, DC: National Academy Press.

Center on Education Policy. (2002). *Changing schools, enduring principles.* Washington, DC: Author.

Clark, T. (2000). *Virtual high schools: State of the states.* Macomb: Western Illinois University, College of Education and Human Services, Center for the Application of Information Technologies.

Collins, A., Brown, J. S., & Newman, S. E. (1989). Cognitive apprenticeship: Teaching the crafts of reading, writing, and mathematics. In L. B. Resnick (Ed.), *Knowing, learning, and instruction: Essays in honor of Robert Glaser* (pp. 453–494). Hillsdale, NJ: Lawrence Erlbaum Associates.

Collison, G., Elbaum, B., Haavind, S., & Tinker, R. (2000). *Facilitating online learning: Effective strategies for moderators.* Madison, WI: Atwood.

Commission on the Future of the Advanced Placement Program. (2001). *Access to excellence: A report of the Commission on the Future of the Advanced Placement Program.* New York: College Board. (Available at: http://cbweb2s.collegeboard.org/ap/pdf/accesstoexcellbk.pdf)

Dede, C. (1998). *Learning with technology: ASCD Yearbook.* Alexandria, VA: Association for Supervision and Curriculum Development.

Farrell, G. M. (1999). *The development of virtual education: A global perspective. A study of current trends in the virtual delivery of education.* Vancouver, British Columbia: Commonwealth of Learning. (ERIC Document Reproduction Service No. ED 432 668)

Flisi, M. (2001, April 26). eLearning is burgeoning. *eBusiness Trends.* (Available at: http://www.itworld.com/nl/ebus_trends/04262001/pf_index.html)

Former ED Sec. Bennett launches online schooling firm. (2001, February). *eSchool News*, p. 14.

Gewertz, C. (2001, August 8). Study estimates 850,000 U.S. children schooled at home. *Education Week, 20*(43), 12.

Harasim, L., Hiltz, S., Teles, L., & Turoff, M. (1995). *Learning networks*. Cambridge, MA: MIT Press.

Hiltz, S. (1995). *The virtual classroom: Learning without limits via computer networks*. Norwood, NJ: Ablex.

Hittelman, M. (2001). *Distance education report, August 2001: California community colleges, fiscal years 1995–1996 through 1999–2000*. Sacramento: California Community Colleges, Office of the Chancellor. (ERIC Document Reproduction Service No. ED 456 886)

Hussar, W. J. (1999). Predicting the need for newly hired teachers in the United States to 2008–09. Washington, DC: National Center for Education Statistics.

Information Infrastructure Task Force. (1993). *The national information infrastructure: Agenda for action*. Washington, DC: U.S. Government Printing Office.

Institute for Higher Education Policy. (1999). *What's the difference? A review of contemporary research on the effectiveness of distance learning in higher education*. Washington, DC: Author.

Institute for Higher Education Policy. (2000). *Quality on the line: Benchmarks for success in Internet-based distance education*. Washington, DC: National Education Association. (Available at: http://www.nea.org/he/abouthe/Quality.pdf)

International Society for Technology in Education. (2000). *National educational technology standards for teachers*. Eugene, OR: Author. (Available at: http://www.iste.org)

Knowlton, D. (2000). A theoretical framework for the online classroom: A defense and delineation of a student-centered pedagogy. *New Directions for Teaching and Learning, 84*, 5–14.

Kozma, R., & Schank, P. (1998). Connecting with the 21st century: Technology in support of educational reform. In C. Dede (Ed.), *Learning with technology: ASCD Yearbook* (pp. 3–30). Alexandria, VA: Association for Supervision and Curriculum Development.

KPMG Consulting. (2001). *Cyber charter schools review*. Pennsylvania Department of Education. (Available at: http://www.pde.psu.edu/cybercs/cybercsrev.html)

Kurzweil, R. (1999). *The age of spiritual machines: When computers exceed human intelligence*. New York: Penguin Putnam.

Means, B., & Olson, K. (1995). *Technology's role in education reform*. Menlo Park, CA: SRI International.

Morabito, M. G. (1997). *Foundations of distance education*. East Rochester, NY: CAL Campus. (ERIC Document Reproduction Service No. ED 412 357) Available at: www.calcampus.com

NASBE Study Group on e-Learning. (2001). *Any time, any place, any path, any pace: Taking the lead on e-learning policy*. Alexandria, VA: National Association of State Boards of Education.

National Center for Education Statistics (NCES). (2000). *Distance education at post-*

secondary education institutions: 1997–98. Washington, DC: U.S. Department of Education.

National Center for Education Statistics (NCES). (2001a). *Internet access in U.S. public schools and classrooms: 1994–2000.* Washington, DC: U.S. Department of Education.

National Center for Education Statistics (NCES). (2001b). *Revenues and expenditures for public elementary and secondary education: School year 1998–99.* Washington, DC: U.S. Department of Education.

National Education Association (NEA). (1999). *Technology brief: Distance education.* (Available at: http://www.nea.org/cet/briefs/16.html)

Newburger, E. (2001). *Home computers and Internet use in the United States: August 2000.* Washington, DC: U.S. Census Bureau.

Norman, D. A. (1988). *The psychology of everyday things.* New York: Basic Books.

Palloff, R., & Pratt, K. (1999). *Building learning communities in cyberspace: Effective strategies for the online classroom.* San Francisco, CA: Jossey-Bass.

Palloff, R., & Pratt, K. (2001). *Lessons from the cyberspace classroom: The realities of online teaching.* San Francisco, CA: Jossey-Bass.

Pellegrino, J., Glaser, R., & Chudowsky, N. (2001). *Knowing what students know: The science and design of educational assessment.* Washington, DC: National Academy Press.

President's Committee of Advisors on Science and Technology. (1997). *Report to the president on the use of technology to strengthen K–12 education in the United States.* Washington, DC: U.S. Government Printing Office.

Reich, R. (1991). *The work of nations.* New York: Knopf.

Resnick, L. (1987). Learning in school and out. *Educational Researcher, 16*(9), 13–20.

Roschelle, J., & Pea, R. (1999, June–July). Trajectories from today's WWW to a powerful educational infrastructure. *Educational Researcher, 28*(5), 22–25.

Rose, L., & Gallup, A. (2001, September). The 33rd annual Phi Delta Kappa/Gallup Poll of the public's attitudes toward the public schools. *Phi Delta Kappan, 83*(1), 41–48.

Secretary's Commission on Necessary Skills. (2000). [Website]. Johns Hopkins University Institute for Policy Studies. Retrieved Dec. 11, 2001 from the World Wide Web: www.scans.jhu.edu.

Simonson, M., Smaldino, S., Albright, M., & Zvacek, S. (2000). *Teaching and learning at a distance: Foundations of distance education.* Upper Saddle River, NJ: Merrill.

Southern Regional Education Board. (2000). *Principles of good practice: The foundation for quality of the electronic campus of the Southern Regional Education Board.* (Available at: http://www.electroniccampus.org/student/srecinfo/publications/principles.asp)

Steinberg, J. (2000, July 7). As teacher in the classroom, Internet needs fine-tuning. *New York Times.* (Available at: http://www.nytimes.com)

Szuhaj, P. K., & Ledger, M. A. (2001, Winter). America clicks. *Trust: The Pew Charitable Trusts, 4*(1), 14–19.

Tidewater Community College, Office of Institutional Effectiveness. (2001). *Tidewater Community College distance learning report.* Norfolk, VA: Author. (ERIC Document Reproduction Service No. ED 456 877)

Tinker, R. (1996). *The Virtual High School Consortium: A cooperative for sharing educational resources on the Internet* (Proposal to the U.S. Department of Education). Concord, MA: Concord Consortium.

Trotter, A. (2001a, January 10). Army's new cyber-school opens doors for online learners. *Education Week, 20*(16), 6.

Trotter, A. (2001b, January 24). Cyber learning at Online High. *Education Week, 20*(19), 28–33.

Trotter, A. (2001c, October 24). Cyber schools carving out charter niche. *Education Week, 21*(8), 1, 21.

Twigg, C. (1994, November/December). National learning infrastructure: Part 3. *Educom Review, 29*(6), 1–5.

Tyack, D., & Cuban, L. (1995). *Tinkering toward Utopia: A century of public school reform.* Cambridge, MA: Harvard University Press.

UCCP Program. (2001). *Status report: September 2001.* (Available at: http://www.uccp.org/docs/Sept%20Status.pdf)

U.S. Department of Education. (1996). *Getting America's students ready for the 21st century: Meeting the technology literacy challenge.* Washington, DC: U.S. Government Printing Office.

U.S. Department of Education. (2001). *ED Review, October 26, 2001.* Washington, DC: Author.

Van Dusen, G. (2000). *Digital dilemma: Issues of access, cost, and quality in media-enhanced and distance education.* San Francisco, CA: Jossey-Bass.

Web-Based Education Commission. (2000). *The power of the Internet for learning: Moving from promise to practice.* Washington, DC: U.S. Department of Education.

Weston, K. R. (1997). *UNIVAC: The Paul Revere of the computer revolution* (Available at: http://ei.cs.vt.edu/~history/UNIVAC.Weston.html)

Winograd, K. (March/April 2002). ABCs of the Virtual High School. *The technology source.* (Available at: http://ts.mivu.org)

Yamashiro, K., & Zucker, A. (1999). *An expert panel review of the quality of Virtual High School courses: Final report.* Menlo Park, CA: SRI International.

Zakon, R. (2001). *Hobbes' Internet timeline v5.3.* (Available at: http://www.zakon.org/robert/internet/timeline/#Growth)

INDEX

ABOUT THE AUTHORS

Dr. Andrew Zucker is an associate director of the Center for Education Policy at SRI International (*www.sri.com/policy/cep*), where he has co-directed SRI's 5-year evaluation of the Concord Consortium-Hudson Public Schools Virtual High School, and supervised a large national study of professional development and teachers' uses of technology for the U.S. Department of Education. He and his colleagues at SRI's Center for Technology in Learning recently developed *Math Insight*, multimedia educational software for middle schools. Dr. Zucker also co-directed a national evaluation by SRI of statewide reform efforts in mathematics and science education. He wrote the chapter on mathematics in *Teaching for Meaning in High-Poverty Classrooms* (Teachers College Press, 1995) and serves on the editorial panel of the *Journal for Research in Mathematics Education*. Before joining SRI in 1986, Dr. Zucker worked for the U.S. Department of Education. Earlier, he worked as a teacher of mathematics, science, and computers and was director of a school computer center. Dr. Zucker holds a doctoral degree from Harvard, a master's from Stanford, and was an Education Policy Fellow at the Institute for Educational Leadership in Washington, DC.

Dr. Robert Kozma is a Principal Scientist and Fulbright Senior Specialist at SRI International's Center for Technology in Learning. His research expertise includes international educational technology research, the evaluation of technology-based reform, and the design of advanced interactive multimedia systems. He has directed or co-directed over 20 projects, including SRI's evaluation of the Virtual High School, and authored or co-authored more than 40 articles and books. Dr. Kozma has consulted with Ministries of Education in Singapore, Thailand, and Chile on the use of technology to improve educational systems.

Dr. Camille Marder is a Senior Social Science Researcher at SRI International. A contributor to SRI's National Longitudinal Transition of Special Education Youth 10 years ago, Dr. Marder recently rejoined SRI's Center for Education and Human Services to work on the Second National Longitudinal Transition of Special Education Youth and two related studies for the U.S. Department of Education. In the interim, as associate director of SRI's Higher Education Policy and Evaluation Program, Dr. Marder examined reforms in postsecondary education, directing an evaluation of the National Science Foundation's Undergraduate Faculty Enhancement program. She also examined K–12 reform efforts in various states and in several developing countries, focusing especially on the roles of technology and professional development. Dr. Marder received her M.A. and Ph.D. in sociology from Stanford University.

Dr. Louise Yarnall is a Research Social Scientist at SRI International in Menlo Park, CA, where she designs classroom learning assessments, evaluations of educational reform, and educational software content and interfaces. A co-designer of Team Lab, handheld software to support classroom assessment of student group work, her recent software design work has focused on working with South Carolina teachers to develop science inquiry assessments on portable handheld devices. Her evaluation work includes the K–12 science inquiry program Global Learning and Observations to Benefit the Environment (GLOBE) and the Bill and Melinda Gates Foundation's small high school school reform study. A former full-time journalist, Dr. Yarnall's work has appeared in the Los Angeles Times and New York Times. She takes a keen interest in literacy education, particularly as it relates to developing students' skills of analysis and thought regarding political affairs. Yarnall recently earned her doctorate at UCLA's Graduate School of Education and Information Studies.